Chance and willpower

Chance and willpower

Lives in France, Bigorre and the Americas from the seventeenth to the twentieth century

Monograph

Ed2

Henri CESTIA

Pursuant to Art. L.137-2.-I. of the Intellectual Property Code, any reproduction and/or disclosure of parts of the work exceeding the volume provided for by law is expressly prohibited.

© Henri CESTIA, 2024Translated from the French by Microsoft Translator
Cover drawing: Thomas CESTIA
Photos: Author's family album
Edition: BoD · Books on Demand GmbH, In de Tarpen 42, 22848 Norderstedt (Germany)
Printing: Libri Plureos GmbH, Friedensallee 273, 22763 Hamburg (Germany)

ISBN : 978-2-3224-7797-5
Legal deposit : December 2024

Is remercie:
- My parents who initiated the genealogical research of the Cestia branch of our family,
- My wife who for more than 15 years has been bringing her opinion and remarks to my work,
- Lionel Dupont who passed on to me the history of my family in Uruguay,
- My Luciani cousins who opened their shoebox full of memories to me,
- Raymonde Aubian, and pays tribute to him. A tireless volunteer at the departmental archives of Tarbes, she always kindly sent me the requested records of acts,
- The many genealogists met on the web: Jean Paul Abadie, Georges Ano, Simone Arrizabalaga, Christian Auguin, Jean Borderes, Sandrine Braun, Laetizia Castellani, Michèle Cazaux, Thierry Cenac, Burton Cestia, Christine Cestia, Michel Cestia, Martine Dagnino, Dominique Delluc, Paulette Faivre, Pierre Frustier, Bernard Herrou, Jean Yves Herve, Roland Larre, Jeannette Legendre, Ana Malbos, Myriam Managau, Alain Medina, Jean Marc Nougues, Jean-François Quarre, Nadine Sahoune, Christine Saintupery, Michel Sauvée, Roberte Thomaset, with whom we have shared our genealogies since 1999.

My passion for genealogy is not motivated by the compulsive establishment of lists of ancestors, but is expressed in a micro-history approach [1], a way of encountering History through the life stories of ordinary people with sometimes fascinating destinies who have all made History.

The surname Cestia is rare; few people today bear this surname, which aroused my curiosity to know its origin, especially since some hypotheses proposed by linguists are hardly rewarding, ... simple-minded, stupid [2].

Satisfying this double curiosity, one concerning micro-history, the other concerning the surname Cestia, I try, quite simply, by following the common thread of the transmission of a surname, to tell stories, to tell the story of lives, families and terroirs, to give life to people that History has not retained... and perhaps, in the end, to better understand History.

With this book, I do not wish to drape myself in the past glory of some of my ancestors, but neither do I wish to put up with the faults of others. My only guide is to bear witness to their lives.

Genealogical research is sometimes similar to a police investigation. From an event found, sometimes by chance, for example the presence of a person on a boarding list, we look for other elements related to the information found. To do this, it is necessary to explore different available archives to find additional data and thus discover the events of the person's life. But success is not 100% assured. Thus, my research on 604 people listed between the seventeenth and twentieth centuries could not be satisfactorily completed for 73 people, i.e. 12%.

This book is not a novel. He relates proven facts. However, some filiations, particularly in the seventeenth century, are only very likely. The information provided without the *"proofs"* by friendly genealogists has been verified.

The first edition, the draft of this one, told the story of the Cestia in reverse, that is, in the way genealogists do their research, that is, starting with their parents, then their grandparents and so on going back in time. I was criticized for this deliberate choice on my part. Indeed, it detracted from the clarity of the story. The second

---

1 Influenced by Edward Palmer Thompson, microhistory suggests that historians abandon the study of masses or classes to focus on individuals. By following the thread of an individual's particular destiny, we shed light on the characteristics of the world around him. Italian micro-historians advocate a reduction in scale, in order to examine the phenomena under a magnifying glass (Wikipedia).

2 The Dauzat dictionary of surnames establishes a link between Cestia and the term crestian, which means "Christian" in Occitan. In the feminine, crestiana. All its forms have the general meaning blessed by God, simple-minded. Linguists also teach us that the word Christian gave rise to the word moron...

criticism was the absence of an index of the people cited, an index so dear to genealogists!

In the present edition I have put the story right, I mean that the story is chronological. An index of the names cited can be found at the end of the book. Genealogists will find on my website for all the people mentioned in the index all the genealogical sources, various acts, proofs of filiation and other information.

Finally, to enhance the reading of the book, I drew on the family's photo albums.

http://www.genea-cestia.fr/

Summary

1. Origin and history of the surname Cestia 11
2. From 1600 to 1700 21
3. From 1700 to 1750 25
4. Lescurry from 1639 to 1891 32
5. From 1750 to 1800 working to survive 39
6. Slavery in France in the nineteenth century 53
7. Migrating to escape poverty 62
8. From 1800 to 1850, getting out of poverty 66
9. Conscription in France from 1789 to 1998 86
10. from 1850 to 1900 88
11. The Cestia in France in the twentieth century 102
12. from 1900 to 1946 Felix Cestia 104
13. 1914-1918 Emile and Jules Cestia 111
14. 1914-1918 Juan-Carlos Dupont 124
15. The Cestia in France from 1900 to 1946 145
16. The Cestia in the United States of America from 1900 to 1946 148
17. Conclusion 150
18. Alphabetical index of individuals cited 151

1. Origin and history of the surname Cestia

The search for the origin of a surname is a complex subject. Genealogy allows us to know the ancient form of the surname. Linguists provide interpretations that I propose to compare with the contributions of the genealogy of the Cestia and the toponymic study.

According to linguists

The Etymological Dictionary of Gascon Surnames by Michel Grosclaude 2003, indicates for the surname Cestia: "Rare surname. In Pyrénées-Atlantiques: 5 outbreaks in Oloron, Nay, Moumour and Pau. Obscure: Perhaps from the Latin man's name Sextianus? Or contraction of Sebastian? – Sestia. Spelling restored: Sestian Sestiaa. »

The linguist Albert Dauzat [3] proposes another hypothesis. According to him, this surname would have its origin in the populations of cagots present in the south-west of France in the Middle Ages. Cagots were people belonging to certain disadvantaged social groups grouped in isolates in the high valleys of the central and western Pyrenees that were difficult to access. The cagots were victims of various discriminations, in the church in particular a stoup was reserved for them. Thus, according to him, the names of Chrétien and Chrestien attributed to these populations give Chrestia and in Béarnais Crestiaa.

The term Crestian means *"Christian"* in Occitan. In the feminine, Crestiana. All these forms have the general meaning of being blessed by God, simple-minded. In the Valais, Chrétien gave the surname Crétin, a surname that is still very common today, especially in France in the departments of Jura and Doubs, but also gave the word of the French language crétin.

According to genealogy

Genealogy tells us that all the current bearers of the surname Cestia have Guilhem Sestian as their ancestor , Arnauld Sestian , Bernard Sestian , Guilhaume Sestian or Pierre Jean Sestian -, owners of land and houses in Lescurry. Thus, Sestian is the old form of the current surname Cestia. These five Sestians, who can be assumed to belong to the same family, were, around 1600, well-established owners in the village of Lescurry. Between them, they own 10% of the land and real estate in the village. It therefore seems likely that they have been present in this village of Lescurry for at least a few generations.

---

3 Albert Dauzat, "Etymological Dictionary of Family Names and First Names of France", 1973, Larousse.

The hypothesis put forward by the linguist Albert Dauzat mentioned above does not stand up to the analysis of the facts, because there are between the mountains and Lescurry, where the surname appears before 1600, many other villages or Sestians could have taken root, which is not the case. Indeed, many systematic records of parish registers are available for the seventeenth and eighteenth centuries. On a database [4] of 35,000 records concerning 300 communes in the Hautes-Pyrénées department [5], there are no Sestian or other variants elsewhere than in the villages near Lescurry. The trail of the Pyrenean mountains being ruled out, linguists direct us to a Latin name, which is in line with the toponymic approach.

Indeed, the proximity of Lescurry to the lands of Sestias leads us to consider the hypothesis that our distant ancestors of Lescurry originated from the hamlet of Cestias. The migration of one or more inhabitants of the hamlet of Cestias to Lescurry could have occurred in the fifteenth or early sixteenth century.

These migrants from Cestias were then referred to by a patronymic name that designated their village of origin, Sestias, Sestianum in the form that designates the origin. Which gives in Gascon Sestian. Indeed, in Latin, the last syllable never bears the tonic accent, so disappears when you switch from Latin to Occitan. Also, words that end in Latin with -anum, end in Occitan with -an. [6]. Thus was probably born the surname Sestian, whose current form is Cestia or Cestiaa.

The distant ancestors of the Cestia were not always called Cestia. Indeed, it was the appearance of the family record book around 1877 that made it possible in France to transmit family names without alteration from one generation to the next. Until then, parish or republican civil status was established on the basis of verbal declarations, which therefore led to variations, sometimes significant, in the way surnames were written, especially in periods when few people knew how to write their name.

The graph below represents the census (number of bearers of the name in ordinate) of the different forms of the surname Cestia, a census established on the basis of the

---

4 http://jme.webhop.net/relhp65/index.php

5 Statistically, the 300 municipalities observed are a representative sample of the 343 municipalities in the department. Statisticians agree that a sample size of 300, which represents 88% of the population studied, is representative of the population studied with a margin of error close to 2%.

6 Footnote by Michel Grosclaude – Toponymy on the website of the Hautes-Pyrénées departmental archives.

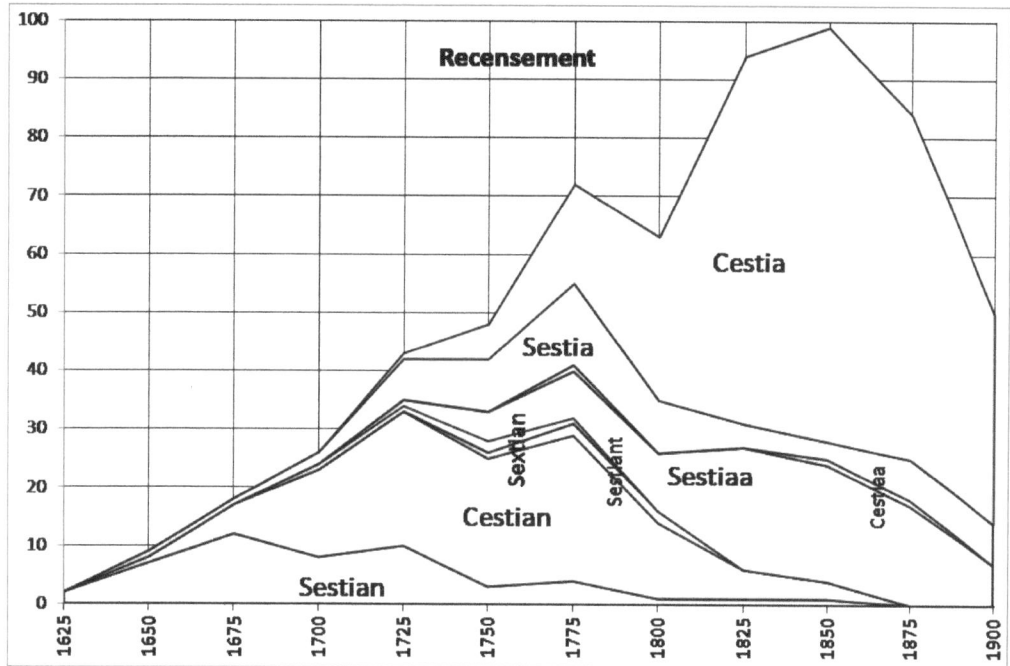

cards compiled during my research. We observe the replacement of the initial letter S by the letter C, except in the regional form Sestiaa in Nay, and then the gradual disappearance of the ending in *"an"*.

Without it being a certainty, these figures tell us that these surnames will, sooner or later, join the long list of surnames that have disappeared, especially in France.

According to toponymy

The hamlet of Cestias is distant from Lescurry by a walking route of about 19 kilometres, which represents about 4h30mn of walking.

The Gallo-Roman and medieval history of this hamlet provide us with interesting information. Concerning Sestias, Charles Brun points out the presence, at the beginning of the century [7], of "a castle at the highest point of the place, 50 metres to the west of the farm. The road to Miélan passes right in the middle of the castle site. We can still see some traces of the ditches which allow us to see that the castle formed a quadrilateral of about 30 to 40 meters on each side."

---

7 Quoted by Stéphane Abadie, Brun, ibidem, pp. XXX-XXXII and 46. Nothing remains of this site, it seems.

Gallo-Roman period

According to Stéphane Abadie [8], "The district of Sestias, now Cestias, is located in the western part of the municipal territory. This toponym comes from the Gallo-Latin surname Sestianus (Sestius), identified by some authors with the location of a villa of Sulpicius Severus in Late Antiquity, and where Saint Justin was buried9. However, no Gallo-Roman finds have confirmed this hypothesis. »

Rome – Cestia Pyramid

Cestius is a Roman surname. Sextus is a Roman given name. In Roman times, Cestius is mentioned by Cicero in his discourse on Flaceus and in his letter to Atticus. The third Cestius, also mentioned by Cicero, was Gaiius Cestius praetor (magistrate) in 44 B.C. From this time, there remains in Rome, at the end of there via Cestia, the mausoleum of the magistrate Gaius Cestius who died in 12 BC. This monument is a pyramid covered with marble. "Tomb worthy of a pharaoh" according to the expression of the Michelin Guide of Rome (1988 edition). After Caesar's death, we find a Lucius Cestius praetor whose name appears on an Aureus. On this coin, the bust evokes Africa, and alludes to the role that Lucius Cestius must have played in this country.

At the beginning of our Cestius era coming from Rome, arrived and settled in the south of Gaul near Trie-sur-Baïse. This historical fact is not proven. However, this is a probable hypothesis put forward by the historian Stéphane Abadie in his monograph of the canton of Baïse. It would be necessary to excavate the grounds of the hamlet of Cestias to find out more, and to confirm that it is indeed this Roman surname that gave its name to the current hamlet of Cestias. Until proven otherwise, we will therefore reject this hypothesis.

Medieval period

The old seigniorial castle of Sestias is in the southern part of the current hamlet of Cestias, 1 km north of Lapeyre and 2.2 km from the bastide town of Trie. It is a platform-type fortress resulting from a development by "recutting" the pre-existing relief in order to increase the surface area of the summit platform.

---

8 Stéphane Abadie, "Master's degree in history. Monograph of the canton of Trie-sur-Baïse".

9 Jean Francez, BSR 1973, Sextiacum/ Sestias in Trie-sur-Baïse; Alcide Curie Seimbres, Recherches sur les lieux habités par Sulpice Sévère, 1875

In the Middle Ages, the territory of Sestias was independent. There are several mentions of the lords of Sestias in the cartulary of Berdoues [10] :
- There is mention of one by Guillaume Sestias at the beginning of the thirteenth century. In 1202 the first mention of the Lordship of Sestias (Sestiano family) appears on the Cartulary of Berdoues (act n° 324)
- In 1323, Condorine de Sestias married Géraud d'Esparros. These two names are found in the paréage of Trie.
- In 1331, they sold the land of Sestias to *"the powerful Centulle, Count of Astarac"* for 1,220 livres tournois.
- In 1489, finally, Jean d'Astarac gives in fief to the inhabitants of Trie, the territories of Trie and Maroncères.

The lordship of Sestias belongs to the county of Astarac. The county of Astarac is located in the north-east of the county of Bigorre. In the Middle Ages, relations between the different counties were often conflictual. The counties of Bigorre and Astarac are no exception.

On 25 March 1331, Centule IV bought from Condorine de Sestias and to her husband Geraud of Esparos the land of Sestias for 1,220 livres tournois. Located in the current department of Hautes-Pyrénées, this lordship is located in the centre of a set of lands belonging to the Count of Astarac by the tributes [11] of 23 October 1374 and 3 May 1392. [12]

Condorine from Sestias was lord of Sestias, then Countess of Sestias after her marriage in 1323. The sale of the lands of Sestias in 1331 gave the lordship to Centule IV d'Astarrac who governed the county of Astarac under the tutelage of his mother of Cécile Comminges . In 1489 Jean d'Astarrac is the lord of Sestias.

In the Middle Ages, it was lords and counts who ruled the region. The lords of Sestias built a castle on the highest point of their land, 30 metres wide and 40 metres long. Behind the thick walls of their castle, they had a solid shelter that allowed them to wage war against their neighbours. Condorine from Sestias who was only Lord of Sestias like her father, when she married the young Count of Astarac whose county was located north of Bigorre, became, by her marriage, Countess of Sestias.

---

10 J. Cazauran, *"Le cartulaire de Berdoues",* act 324, p.221 of 1202: Guillelmus Sestianum, sacerdos; idem, act 562 p.386 of 1221: Willemus de Sistian, clericus.

11 In the Middle Ages, vassal homage was the ceremony during which a free man, the vassal, placed himself under the protection of another, more powerful free man, the overlord.

12 Nicolas Guinaudeau, "Seigniorial Fortifications and Gascon Aristocratic Residences between the Tenth and the Sixteenth Century", Thesis Medieval History 2012.

16th and 17th centuries

It was in the sixteenth century that the surname Sestian appeared in the village of Lescurry. Probably because the inhabitants of the lands of Sestias decided to settle a little further south. Sestias gives in Gascon Sestian.

In the first half of the seventeenth century, Lescurry had about 40 houses, 5 of which were houses belonging to the Sestian. The Sestian families then owned about 10% of the houses and land in the village. Some have done well. They are tax collectors. But the others are peasants.

Peasant life was hard in the seventeenth century. In 1694, a terrible famine hit the village hard. Pierre Jean Sestian decided to leave his native village and settle in Nay in the Béarn where the textile trades were developing a lot. Thus Pierre Jean from a family of farmers in Lescurry became a hosiery-maker.

XVIIIth century

In the eighteenth century, the Sestian of Nay were more and more numerous. They were often workers in the nascent textile industry of Nay, which took over from the crafts of the previous period. The surname changes to Cestian, Sestia, Cestia or Sestiaa.

During this time, in 1713 and 1747, Lescurry experienced two terrible years. Other Sestians then left the village of Lescurry to join the Sestian of Nay, while a few others settled on the occasion of a marriage in the neighboring villages of Beccas, Louit, Collongues or Dours in the hope of finding a less thankless land. Villages where they often find a member of their family who is already settled there. The possibility of family solidarity, no doubt a means of coping with the adversity of the century, seems to be a determining factor in the choice of the village of destination.

In the eighteenth century in Lescurry, as everywhere in France among the peasants, life continued to be harsh, despite the slight improvement in living conditions observed from 1725 onwards. The proportion of an age group that exceeds 10 years is only 60%, and only 50% reaches the age of 25. Famines, famines, epidemics transform life into a fight against death. You have to feed yourself to survive. To feed oneself one must work hard, but the climatic conditions must also be favourable. Conditions that are sometimes impossible to meet.

During the second half of the eighteenth century, more and more of the Cestia de Lescurry left their village to settle in villages located north and south of Lescurry and east of a Tarbes-Maubourguet line.

In the eighteenth century, most of the population could not read, write or even sign their name. However, in 1768, Arnauld Cestian (1716-1788) is a tax collector. On the eve of the Jean Cestia Revolution is a member of the municipal body and as such a signatory of the list of grievances of the village of Lescurry which asks for less tax and more freedoms "*which will always be the soul of all commerce*" it reads.

But being a notable of your village does not only have advantages. In 1790, it was decided to make the accounts of the tax collection between 1761 and 1789. It follows that the son of the late Guillaume Cestia had to repay 18 livres tournois, the equivalent of 15 days' wages.

In Nay, the great family of the Cestia has grown even larger. They continue to work in the textile industry but also in the wood industry. Employees of the factories, they lived from day to day, on a meagre salary, legally free but economically dependent. This dependency organized by the kingdom kept them in Nay. No other choice is possible for them.

XIXth century

The nineteenth century is one of extraordinary vitality. The *"industrial revolution"* of the nineteenth century shifted from a predominantly agrarian and artisanal society to a commercial and industrial society. The bearers of the surname Cestia are not immune to this transformation of society. Between 1800 and 1875, nearly 30% of them abandoned the trades of the land in favour of the professions of craftsman, shopkeeper and employee. The Cestia family is present in many villages in the Hautes-Pyrénées and in Nay where they are workers but also craftsmen or shopkeepers.

These changes in jobs are often the consequence of migration. People leave their village to find a better life elsewhere, in the towns and villages of Bigorre to the south of the Gers. But also for the more adventurous to more distant destinations such as Argentina, Uruguay, Louisiana, and the islands of Guadeloupe and Puerto Rico.

The Americas

Jean Alphé Cestia (1834-1860)), originally from Vic-en-Bigorre, migrated to Louisiana at a very young age where he joined a Cestia de Vic. He settled in Abbeville and founded a family that is at the origin of the current presence in Louisiana of the surname Cestia.

Other Cestia, also from Vic, also migrated to Louisiana to work as merchants. Thus, in the nineteenth century in Louisiana, a community of Cestia from Vic-en-Bigorre was formed, well established in trade.

Argentina is also a destination that attracts the Cestia, de Vic, de Dours, Pujo and Lacassagne.

My great-grandfather, Honoré Cestia , decided to go to Uruguay where he became a trader. Around 1900, having become a widower, he returned to the country with his three children. The eldest my grandfather, Felix, is Uruguayan while his two brothers, Emile and Jules, have dual nationality. A detail? No, the rest proves that it is not.

In the second half of the nineteenth century, Uruguay was a popular destination for many French people who found in this country an economic dynamism favourable to rapid success in business.

My great-grandfather's brother, Auguste-Sylvain Cestia who did not want to spend 5 years of his life as a soldier, and possibly go to war, he left for Argentina. Like him, many Cestia are thus declared insubordinate by the military authorities. Auguste-Sylvain died in Buenos Aires in 1897, at the age of 33.

La Guadeloupe

The islands of Guadeloupe and Puerto Rico are also a destination chosen by those who finally aspire to a better life, in order to turn the page on the eighteenth century made of suffering and misfortune. The practice of slavery, which was legal in Guadeloupe until 1848, did not stop them. From 1800 to 1848, this "servile" workforce, according to the term used in population censuses, was the only one available to exploit the dwellings, the name given to the agro-industrial complexes for sugar production. Human rights took a long time to penetrate nineteenth-century society, first with the prohibition of the slave trade, which consisted of going to look for blacks in Africa, then in 1848 with the abolition of the slave trade.

Bertrand Cestia (1805-1876), the son of the butcher of Vic, was the first Cestia to migrate to Guadeloupe where he quickly became successful in the trade. His job as a merchant was to transport the sugar produced to Bordeaux, and to bring clothing, food and agricultural tools from Bordeaux. On the spot, he is also a businessman whose opinion is sought. Three years before his return, in 1833, he bought the estate of St Aunis located in the communes of Vic and Pujo, and a little later became a notable mayor of his commune and a member of the academic society of the Hautes-Pyrénées.

Around 1830 Pierre Cestia and Philippe Cestia de Louit migrated to Guadeloupe, which was experiencing an economic crisis at the time. The revolt of the blacks in the neighboring island of Saint-Domingue led to the independence of part of the island, and the creation of the state of Haiti in 1804. In Guadeloupe, at the same time, the bloody repression of the black uprising discouraged any revolt. The temporary drop in sugar production in Haiti, followed by the resumption of production, caused overproduction in Guadeloupe which, combined with the shortage of slaves, led to serious economic difficulties.

It is in this difficult economic context that Pierre Cestia and Philippe Cestia de Louit arrive in Guadeloupe at Port Louis. There they meet the Fabares de Louit family, an allied family. Fabares Martial is the brother of Jeanne Fabares of Louit, the aunt of the Cestia brothers. In Guadeloupe, Martial Fabares married the heiress of the Dadon estate. It's a big house. Pierre and Philippe Cestia are therefore not arriving without local support.

As soon as he arrived, Pierre Cestia is in business with Cestia Bertrand about a 160-hectare house in the commune of Sainte Rose. But this agreement, sealed before a notary, only lasted a few months. The termination of the agreement allows Pierre Cestia to be compensated for an amount of 5,406 francs, a sum that represents more than 10% of the initial purchase price of the house.

As for Philippe, he was first a shopkeeper and then a landowner, which allowed him to redress the financial situation of his wife Marie-Anne-Zeline Dumornay-Matignon after his marriage born in Guadeloupe, daughter of a settler and widow without children.

In 1843, an earthquake almost completely destroyed Pointe-à-Pitre, located 30 km south of Port-Louis. An ordeal that adds to the difficulties already present on the island. It was then that another Philippe Cestia , my grandfather, Bernard says in his family, joins his two brothers in Guadeloupe. The three brothers were quickly home managers. Philippe is also the manager of a very large 280-hectare house belonging to an owner who has returned to Gironde.

At the time of the abolition, in 1848, Philippe owned 23 slaves for which he was compensated by the state, which allowed him to repay a debt contracted with Despalanques de Vic, a former associate of Bertrand Cestia .

With the abolition of slavery, Guadeloupe's years of economic prosperity came to an end. Many decide to return but the three Cestia brothers decide to stay.

In 1855, Philippe died in Port-Louis without descendants, aged 46. He leaves a widowed wife for the second time. Philippe, known as Bernard, did not stay on the island very long. After his brother's death, he returned home after having previously received the colonial indemnity for the few slaves he had invested in to work on his brother's dwelling. In November 1856 in Louit, Philippe Cestia, known as Bernard, who now called himself an annuitant, married Magdelaine Dortignac who is 19 years old. He is 41 years old… Elected mayor of Louit in 1865, re-elected in 1870, he remained mayor until his death in 1874.

In 1860, a Cestia from Vic, François, migrated at a very young age before the military census of 20-year-old men, a census to which he did not appear. He was therefore declared insubordinate. But a little later he could be exempted from military service because of a disability. In Guadeloupe, he married Marie Cécile Eugénie Aquart-Pieton daughter of Eugène Pieton, sugar industrialist. Before his marriage to Modestine Aquart, Eugène Pieton had an affair with a slave woman who bore him three children whom he recognized in 1833. The mother and her children as well as the grandmother, who was obviously also a slave, were then freed.

Puerto Rico

On the neighboring island of Puerto Rico, there are the first cousins of the Cestia de Louit brothers. They are Pierre Cestia and Catherine Cestia , the children of Martial Cestia and Jeanne Fabares . Pierre is a doctor. They settled in Mayaguez, at the western end of the island. Shortly after his arrival, Pierre met his first cousin in Guadeloupe during a financial transaction involving a large sum of money. At that time, the financing of economic activity was mainly done by family or friends and not by banks as is the case today. In 1843, Catherine Cestia married Angelo Toussaint Giorgi from Farinole in Corsica. It was there that she retired after her time in Puerto Rico.

Thus, in the first half of the nineteenth century, the Cestia formed a family and business clan on the islands, an essential condition for success.

The twentieth century

The world wars were two terrible trials for this period which were also an opportunity for global solidarity to defend Europe against the Germans. Cestia from Louisiana participated in this surge of solidarity and came to defend France in the two world wars. During the first conflict, they fought alongside Jules Cestia and Emile Cestia that they do not know, without knowing, no doubt, that they are defending the land of their ancestors. This is also the fight of Juan-Carlos Dupont who came from Montevideo at a very young age to defend France *"His second homeland"* in his own words. He was just 17 years old, and the military authorities in Tarbes did not agree to enlist him. He had to wait for his parents to sign an authorization, which they eventually did. He can then fight. He becomes a man, he says. He was decorated with the Croix de Guerre.

Two of the three brothers who returned from Uruguay with their father Honoré Cestia are mobilized. Jules Cestia will return from the war with decorations, Emile Cestia he died for France. He leaves a widow and a daughter. Felix Cestia who is Uruguayan is not mobilized. France wins the war, but widespread misfortune makes many losers.

And then 30 years later, it's war again. My grandfather, Felix Cestia , who had become a diplomat, was driven out of France by the Germans. His wife remains alone in Marseille. His son, who voluntarily became French, fought in the war and returned with medals that attested to his courage. His uncle André Cestia , son of Honoré and his second wife Anna, was mobilized. He died for France in Vienne-le-Château on 11 June 1940.

2. From 1600 to 1700

Before 1650, the surname Cestia is present only in Lescurry. In fact, it is rather the surname Sestian, which is the oldest form of the surname Cestia.

Jeanne Sestian

Jeanne Sestian is the last encounter on my genealogical journey that goes back in time from 1946 to 1600. We would like to know more, unfortunately it is here that our time machine runs out of fuel, I mean out of archival documents to feed the machine. But dear reader, this is where the story of the Cestia begins for you.

Jeanne Sestian dit Peyrou would have been born in 1586, if we are to believe her death certificate of December 9, 1676 which indicates the age of 90 years. A very surprising age at a time when very few people know their age. As proof of this, I have the statistics below that I have established on the basis of the ages declared at the time of Lescurry's deaths between 1660 and 1800. We see that from the age of 40 onwards, deaths occur mainly at 45, 50, 55 years of age, etc. These round numbers show that people have a very approximate knowledge of their age. So Jeanne Sestian was probably born towards the very end of the sixteenth century.

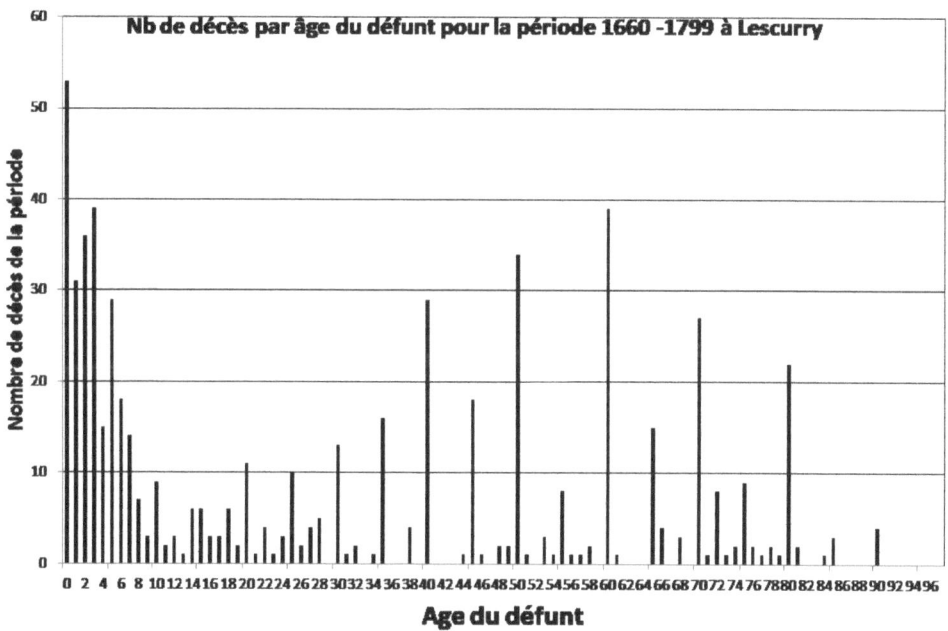

Pierre Sestian

Let's get on our bike one last time to go back in time to meet Pierre Sestian. His wife is Anne Marie Lespiau with whom he had 3 children between 1636 and 1648. The eldest is Jean Sestian Coutillou owner. Then came Bertrande (1642-1707) who married Jean Casaux with whom she had 4 children between 1671 and 1681. Then comes Gabrielle who marries Jean Costabadie with whom she had 10 children between 1671 and 1684.

The Sestian owners

According to the terrier of Lescurry established in 1677, there are about 40 houses, of which, according to the terms used in this document, are *"kept and possessed"* by the Sestian. The agricultural land, woods or wasteland of the inhabitants of the village of Lescurry is estimated at a total of about 1,000 newspapers, i.e. in current unit 350 ha, including 31 ha for the 5 Sestian owners. This inventory of the land owned by the inhabitants of the village does not describe that of the Lord of the village, Philippe de Podenas and his wife Louyse Montbartsier. By difference, the surface area of the seigniorial estate can be estimated at about 150 ha.

The Sestian landowners in the second half of the seventeenth century were:

- Arnaud Sestian (1635-1681) known as Berne which owns about 4 ha of land. He has, with his wife Jeanne Abadie, 3 children between 1658 and 1663 including Bernard whose descendants settled in Nay.
- Jean Sestian Coutillou (1636-1726) who is the son of Pierre Sestian. He owns about 7 ha of land. Between 1652 and 1680, he and his wife Marguerite Laforgue, 8 children, 6 of whom reached adulthood and 5 of whom bore him offspring.
- Guilhem Sestian (1638–1713) which owns about 6 ha of land. Between 1660 and 1690, he had 3 children with his wife Bernarde, 2 of whom gave him descendants
- Sestian Guilhaume (1642-1726) known as Bernis or Bicata which owns about 6 ha of land. In 1672 and 1677, he had a relationship with Jeanne Darric, 2 children including Pierre Jean Sestian who gave him a large number of descendants in Nay.
- Bernard Sestian (1646-1691) known as Camus which owns about 9 ha of land. Between 1665-1691, he had 3 children with Marie Marthe Laforgue, 2 of whom reached adulthood and gave him descendants.

Between 1650 and 1700 the surname Cestia was present in Nay and Lescurry.

Nay

The founders of the Cestia de Nay dynasty were Pierre Jean Sestian Dauveille and Bernard Sestian who had a large number of descendants in Nay.

Pierre Jean was born in Lescurry in 1677. In 1694, he resisted the famine that hit his native village hard. So he's someone of a robust nature.

In 1695, he married Anne Pehourtic of a family originally from Bosdaros located about 10 km west of Nay. His marriage and his move to Nay seem to be linked to the emergence of the textile industry in this city. It was at the beginning of the eighteenth century at the time of the concentration in the city center of Nay of the artisanal textile activity present on the outskirts of the city. Thus Pierre Jean from a family of farmers in Lescurry became a hosiery-maker.

Between 1696 and 1720, Pierre Jean Sestian and Anne Pehourtic had 12 children. Their son Jean, a hosiery maker like his father, gave them 14 grandchildren, including 6 boys who ensured the perpetuation of the name in the town of Nay. Their daughter Marie and Anne were married in Nay. One has 4 children and the other 5.

When Pierre Jean Sestian died in 1747, he was a widower, he was 70 years old; which, at the time, was a very rare age. His grandson Jean was only 6 years old at the time. Pierre Jean Sestian did not experience the social success of his grandson, who became, a little later, a merchant and then a merchant.

The second founder of the Cestia de Nay dynasty was Bernard Sestian who was born around 1636 in Lescurry where, with Marie Gardey between 1680 and 1710, he had 4 children, the two eldest of whom settled in Nay.

Lescurry

The village of Lescurry experienced a terrible famine in 1694 which caused 41 deaths, while the village had only experienced a total of 36 deaths during the previous 5 years, and from 1695 to 1699 the parish priest of Lescurry recorded only 15 deaths. Deaths are generally distributed regularly throughout the year, with a lower number in July, and a higher number in October. For the year 1694, it is different. As the graph below shows, deaths occur mainly from March to June, the lean period between harvests. From 1670 to 1694, there were 200 deaths, i.e. an annual average of 8 deaths per year. Over the same period, the number of births was 169, i.e. an annual average of 6.8 births per year. Thus, as we can see, the years 1650 to 1700 were not, for the village of Lescurry, a period of demographic vitality.

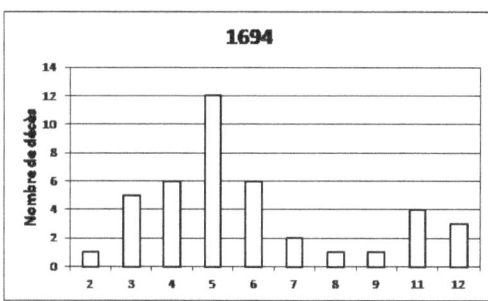

From 1600 to 1700

For the Cestia, the demographic balance is different. Between 1650 and 1694, there were 17 births compared to only 9 deaths for the same period. In 1694 there was only one death in the Cestia family, that of Jean Cestian aged 3 years. The Cestia, 9 in number in 1650, were 21 in 1694. It is understandable, in statistical terms, that the 9 Cestia present in Lescurry in 1650 do not constitute a sample of sufficient size to be representative of the total population of the village.

We can see that in the second half of the seventeenth century, the adversity of existence hits hard but unfairly, the chance of fate presides over the lottery of life.

The demographic vitality of the Cestia is due in particular to Jean Cestian Bicata and his first wife Bernarde Gardey who, between 1692 and 1699, had 5 children, 3 of whom reached adulthood, and who, between 1716 and 1722 with his second wife Catherine Clemens, have 3 children, 2 of whom are reaching adulthood. Four of their children gave them descendants.

Jean Sestian Coutillou and Marguerite Laforgue also contribute to the demographic growth. Between 1652 and 1680, they had 8 children, 6 of whom reached adulthood. Five of their children give them grandchildren. Similarly, between 1681 and 1718, Guilhem Sestian Coutillou and Jeanne Darric have 9 children, 8 of whom are reaching adulthood. Four of their children gave them a large number of descendants. Between 1650 and 1700, there were also many other births in the ten Sestian or Cestia de Lescurry families that contributed to the demographic growth of the Cestia.

3. From 1700 to 1750

In the first half of the eighteenth century, the Cestia were present only in France. America, America... That will be for later.

The textile industry

> Béarn, located northwest of the Pyrenees, is a former sovereign state and then a former French province following its attachment to the Kingdom of France in 1620. From 1751 it was part of the generality of Pau and Auch which administered Béarn, Bigorre, Basse-Navarre, Nébouzan and Soule. Nébouzan is a viscounty created in 1240 by detachment from Comminges. It was made up of several enclaves located in the present-day departments of Hautes-Pyrénées and Haute-Garonne.
>
> A generality is an administrative district of France under the Ancien Régime. (Wikipedia)

The province of Béarn is now the eastern part of the Pyrénées-Atlantiques department.

It was during the eighteenth century that the drapery of Nay, initially made up of craftsmen from the countryside, was partly concentrated in the small town of Nay. Most of the local markets in the textile regions soon became centres of "merchant manufacturers" centralising the production of the countryside. Nay, in the seventeenth century, had about twenty manufacturers. [13]

In the autumn of 1708, the Controller-General of Finances, Nicolas Desmarets, had his subordinates carry out an investigation into the state of the cloth industry in France. This investigation tells us that there were three hundred manufacturers and two hundred and fifty looms in Oloron-Sainte-Marie de Béarn, and that there were in Nay the royal factory Abadie and Saint-Suffrans, the production of which is sold in Béarn, Navarre, the Basque Country, Labourd [14] and Spain.

The Cestia in Nay

In Nay at the beginning of the eighteenth century, the Cestia were Cestian (52%), Sestia (18%), Sestian (10%), Cestia (8%), Sestiaa (8%), and Sestiant or Sextian (5%). The local habit of doubling the final vowel, which has never been in the majority (21% a century later), is still very little adopted.

---

13 Chevalier Michel, "L'industrie textile pyrénéenne et le développement de Lavelanet", Revue géographique des Pyrénées et du Sud-ouest, tome 21, fascicule 1, 1950. pp. 43-60.

14 Labourd: an old feudal fiefdom attached first to Navarre, then to Gascony under the name of Viscount of Labourd and finally to Aquitaine. The territory disappeared with the creation of the Pyrénées-Atlantiques department.

The presence of the Cestia in Nay is closely linked to the textile industry. Pierre Jean Sestian dit Dauveille, a hosiery maker born in Lescurry in 1677, married Anne Pehourtic in Nay in 1695. They had 12 children between 1696 and 1720, including Jean Sestiaa hosiery maker dit Trébayre, born in Nay in 1707 where he married Jeanne Laffont in 1728. They have 14 children, 6 of whom are boys. One of the boys became a merchant and merchant.

Jean Sestian dit Gouailly, merchant born in Lescurry in 1680 married in 1703 in Nay Jeanne Marguerite Anne Gouaille. They had 7 children between 1703 and 1723. Of Jean's second marriage to Marie Anglade 4 children were born between 1724 and 1738, one of whom was a laficier. Jean Sestia, from a family of Lescurry, was born in Nay in 1706. In 1726 he had with Marie Abbadie a son Bernard Laneficier who married Jeanne Marie Lajusa in Nay. They had 8 children between 1762 and 1772, 4 daughters and 4 sons who became laficiaries like their father. These trips between Lescurry and Nay illustrate the attractiveness of this town due most certainly to the textile industry that was born in this small town of Nay at the beginning of the eighteenth century.

The Cestia in Lescurry

The period 1700-1750 was marked at its beginning, in 1713, and at the end, in 1747, by two hecatombs. Lescurry had 21 deaths in 1713 and 19 deaths in 1747, which was considerable for a village of 200 to 250 inhabitants. The average number for the period 1700 to 1750 is 5.6 deaths/year. Despite this, between these two dates, the village experienced a period of 30 years of demographic vitality: the number of marriages per year increased from 2 to 3, and the number of births fell from 7 to 8. The population of the village, which can be estimated at 200 inhabitants in 1700, increased to 250 in 1750. (See below "Lescurry number of inhabitants»)

The graphs below provide an understanding of what happened in 1713 and 1747.

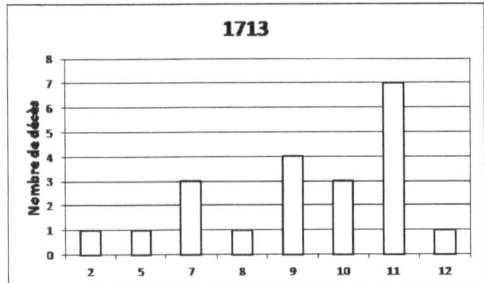 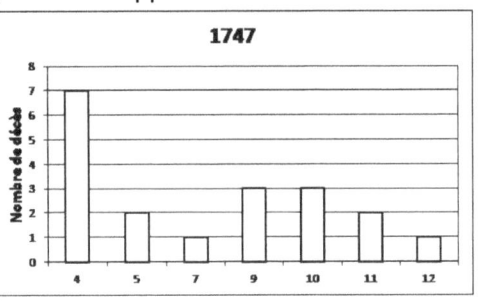

In 1713, the deaths occurred during the bad season. They do not occur in April or May when the lean season between harvests is made. This allows us to put forward the hypothesis of an epidemic, a hypothesis supported by the abundant rains that occurred in 1713 which could have favored the pollution of the water. On the other hand, in 1747, the graph allows us to retain the hypothesis of a famine.

The Cestia de Lescurry do not seem to have escaped these disasters since their number follows the demographic evolution of the village. There were 25 in 1700 and 33 in 1750. Life in Lescurry at the very beginning of the eighteenth century was however hard. However, the Cestia do not leave their village en masse, probably more out of necessity than out of attachment. For the most favoured, they are ploughmen and for those who are less so, brewers who live by the work of their hands. The land sustains them; they cannot leave it except for a few exceptions which concern the youngest, who on the occasion of a wedding pass through a neighboring village.

The weddings of those who leave the village take place in villages near Lescurry: Beccas located 2h30 on foot (12 km), Louit 1 hour (4.7 km), Collongues 1h15 as well as Dours (5.6 km).

- This is the case of Jacques Cestia Coutillou who left his village to marry Jeanne Caubet in 1732 in Beccas with whom he has 4 children.
- This is also the case for three sons of Jean Sestian Bordenave, all three named Jean, the first two of whom married in Louit and had 4 children between 1736 and 1744, the second, 2 children between 1736 and 1744, and the third of whom married in Bayonne where he had 3 children with Marie Baron, but eventually returned to Lescurry where he had 3 more children with his second wife. He then left his job as a gardener to become a winemaker.
- Marie Cestian married in Collongues and had, with Jacques Fontan, 2 children, one in 1712, and the other in 1720.
- Arnaud Sestian married Marie Adamet in Dours where he was born. He became a Saucetter in Dours, like his father. He is an educated and religious person. He was a churchwarden, which meant that he assisted the parish priest in his ministry with material tasks. He had 4 children, one of whom became consul [15].

There are also those who really want to change their lives. This is the case of Jean Sestian who around 1700, married in Nay where he became a merchant. With Jeanne marguerite Anne Gouailles his first wife, he had 7 children between 1702 and 1723, then with Marie Anglade, he had 4 children between 1724 and 1738. This is also the case of Pierre Jean Sestian Dauveille who married in Nay in 1695 where he became a hosiery-maker. He has with Anne Pehourtic 12 children between 1696 and 1720, one of whom became a hosiery maker like him.

But marriage is not the only way to leave one's native village; There is also the military career. This is undoubtedly the case of Joseph Sestian, the son of Bernard and Marie Gardey de Lescurry, who on 1 January 1726 had a daughter in Bruchsal in Germany

---

15 In modern times, a Consul is the equivalent of a municipal elected official of today.

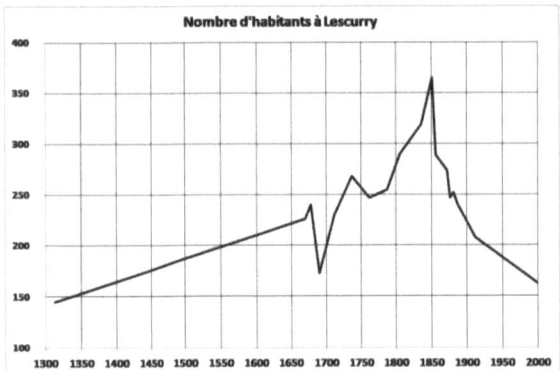

with a certain Franciscae. Was Joseph Sestian a survivor of the defeat at the Battle of Höchstädt, also known as the Battle of Blenheim, on August 13, 1704 who on his way back would have stopped to start a family?

Lescurry number of inhabitants

The graph opposite has been drawn up for the years 1313 and from 1806 to 1999, based on data available on the website of the departmental archives. In the absence of data available for the other years, estimates have been made according to the following calculation formula: the number of inhabitants is equal to the product of the average number of births per year by the average age at death (representative of life expectancy) increased by 3% to take into account the gaps in the registers analysed [16].

The graph thus established shows the two periods of demographic decline: a first decline due to the famines of the late seventeenth century and a second decline in the nineteenth and twentieth centuries, due to technical progress and its consequence, the rural exodus.

The demographic vitality of Lescurry, +0.45% inhabitants/year from 1690 to 1806, is close to that observed in France +0.2% inhabitants/year from 1700 to 1755 and +0.8% from 1755 to 1776, as well as Vauban's national figures, sometimes disputed, of 0.37%/year from 1700 to 1789. [17]

This demographic growth of the eighteenth century continued at the beginning of the nineteenth century until the consequences of technical progress, transport, mechanization of agricultural work, got the better of the development of the village of Lescurry, whose demographic decline continues until recent times.

The Cestia de Louit

It was at the beginning of the eighteenth century that the surname Cestia appeared in Louit. The first Cestia de Louit, which is actually more often Cestian than Cestia, comes from Lescurry. These are the ones who left Lescurry to settle in Louit and start a family there. As we will see below, they are not the only ones to have left Lescurry.

---

16 The so-called *"multiplier" method,* Population and Society N°409, February 2005

17 Léon, "Economies et sociétés préindustrielles 1650-1780". 1970, Armand Collin, p. 214-216.

When Marie Cestian joined his aunt Jeannea in Louit to marry Jacques Fontan, it experienced the slaughter of 1713 in Lescurry. Perhaps she hopes to find a less hard life in Louit. Before her death in 1747, a terrible year, she gave birth to 2 daughters who started a family and had children between 1737 and 1748.

Jean Cestian dit Guilhaumet was born in Lescurry in 1699. When he moved to Louit, he met Marie, his father's first cousin, who was already settled there and married to Jacques Fontan. Jean Cestian married Marguerite Guinle de Louit, with whom he had 4 children between 1736 and 1744. The eldest is Pierre Cestia my grandfather, the father of Jean Cestia, Philippe's father, etc.

Guilhem Cestian was born in Lescurry in 1693. He was the brother of Jean Cestian says Guilhaumet, whom he joins at Louit. Guilhem had, between 1742 and 1745, two children with Marie Luit.

We see it, we see it in the story of this migration between Lescurry and Louit, in this time when life is hard, in the face of adversity, family ties are a way of coping and undoubtedly of being supportive. We stick together and face together, seems to be the rule of life.

The Cestia in Dours

At the beginning of the eighteenth century, the first to leave Lescurry to settle in Dours was Bernard Cestian born in 1692 at Lescurry. He started a family that gave him 11 children, 5 with his first wife Domengea Pére, then 6 with Anne St Upery [18]. His first child to give him grandchildren was Arnaud Sestian who has, with Marie Adamet, 4 children between 1732 and 1755.

Then arrived, another Arnaud Cestian born at Lescurry in 1716. He founded a family in Dours with Jeanne Dardenne. They had 9 children born between 1736 and 1756.

---

18 This surname has undergone many transformations. It became Saint-Ubery and then Sentubery in the nineteenth century.

Location of Nay

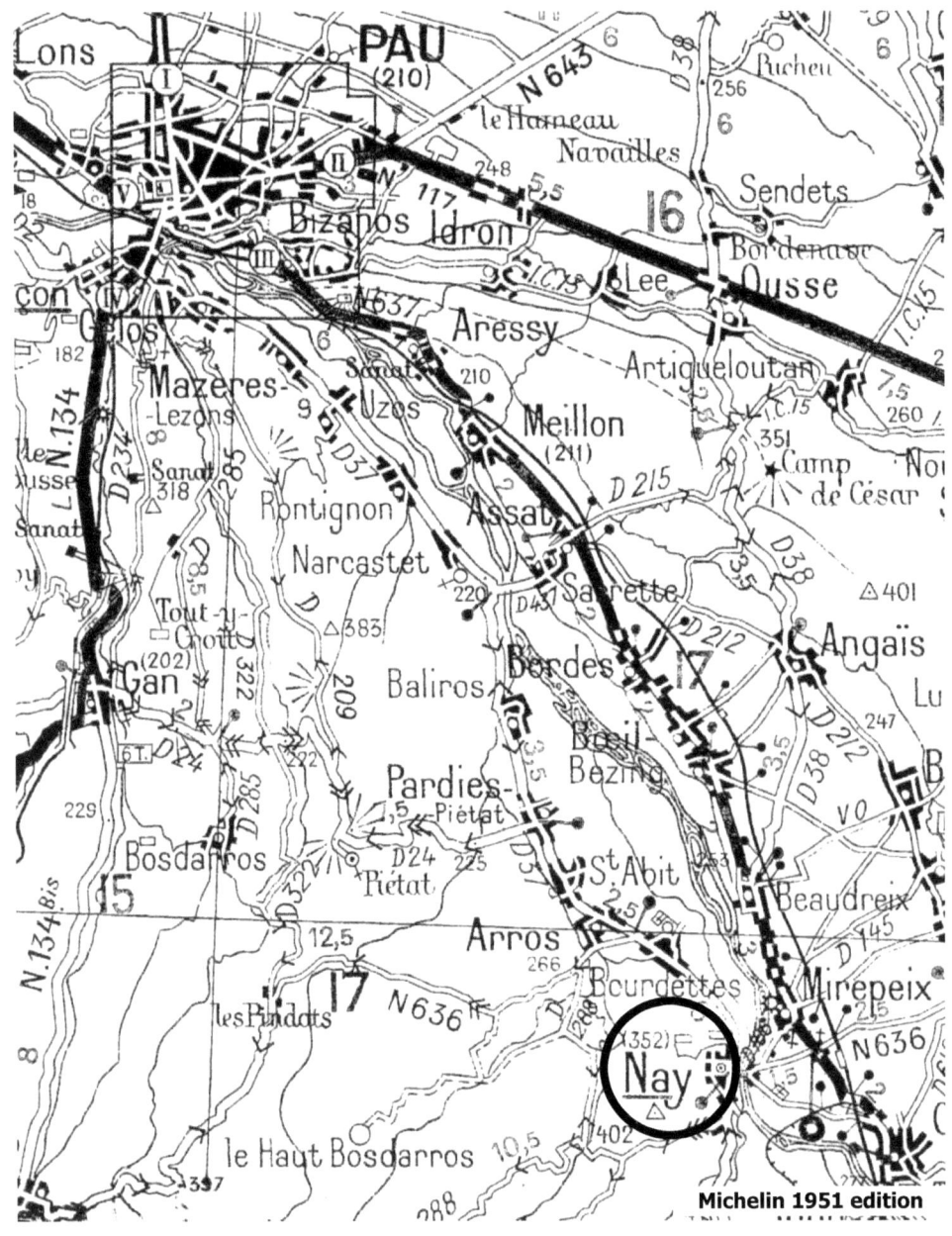

Michelin 1951 edition

Location of Lescurry

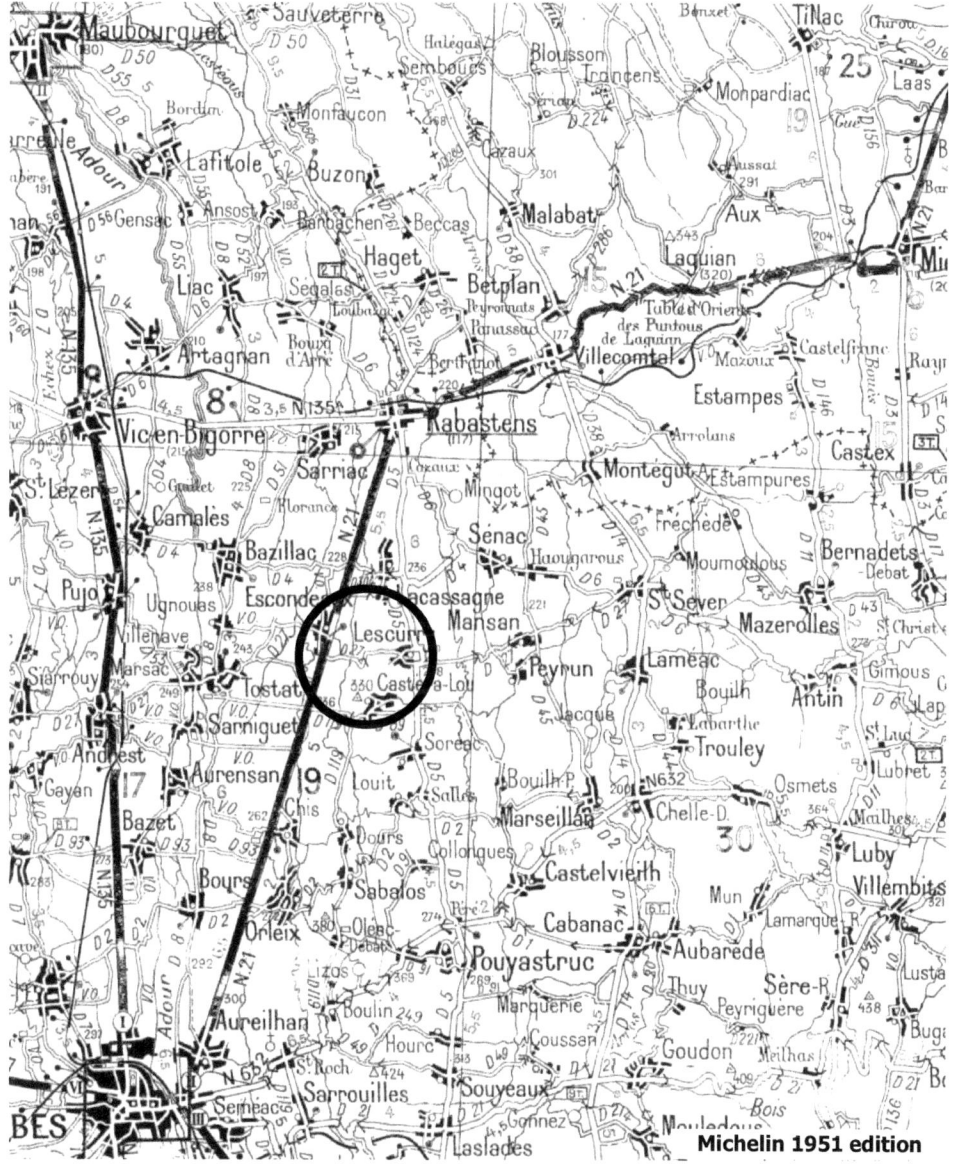

Michelin 1951 edition

4. Lescurry from 1639 to 1891

My research work on the Cestia quickly led me to take a particular interest in the village of Lescurry, and with the help of genealogists who were also volunteers, to carry out a systematic survey of the civil registers of this village over the period 1639-1891.

The statistics compiled using these records concern surnames, occupations and demography, but they also allow economic and social interpretations.

Patronymic

Over the period that covers two and a half centuries, Cestia newborns are the most numerous. They represent almost 8% of births ahead of Darric, Duco, Clemens and Fabares. The village of Lescurry is therefore the village of the Cestia.

Professions

Before the Revolution, civil status records generally did not mention the profession. The statistic, which unsurprisingly indicates that 72% of the population was practised as a farmer, therefore covers the period from 1790 to 1894.

Death

An examination of the death statistics makes it possible to measure the effect of the food crises, famines, shortages and various epidemics which, in Lescurry as elsewhere in France, were numerous in the seventeenth and eighteenth centuries.

"Food crises were observed in Europe in 1660-1662, 1693-1694, 1698-1699" [19]. Lescurry is not spared as can be seen in the graph below.

In France; the great famine of 1693 and 1694 killed nearly 1.7 million French people. In Lescurry the years 1693 and 1694 were terrible. Lescurry resisted this famine until March 1694. But from March to June, it is a hecatomb for the youngest and the oldest.

In the eighteenth century, the incomes of farmers were low and precarious. Royal taxes and seigneurial rights weighed heavily. Climatic variations that lead to poor harvests then produce great difficulties.

---

19 Léon P, "*Economies et sociétés préindustrielles 1650-1780*", 1970, Armand Colin, page 49.

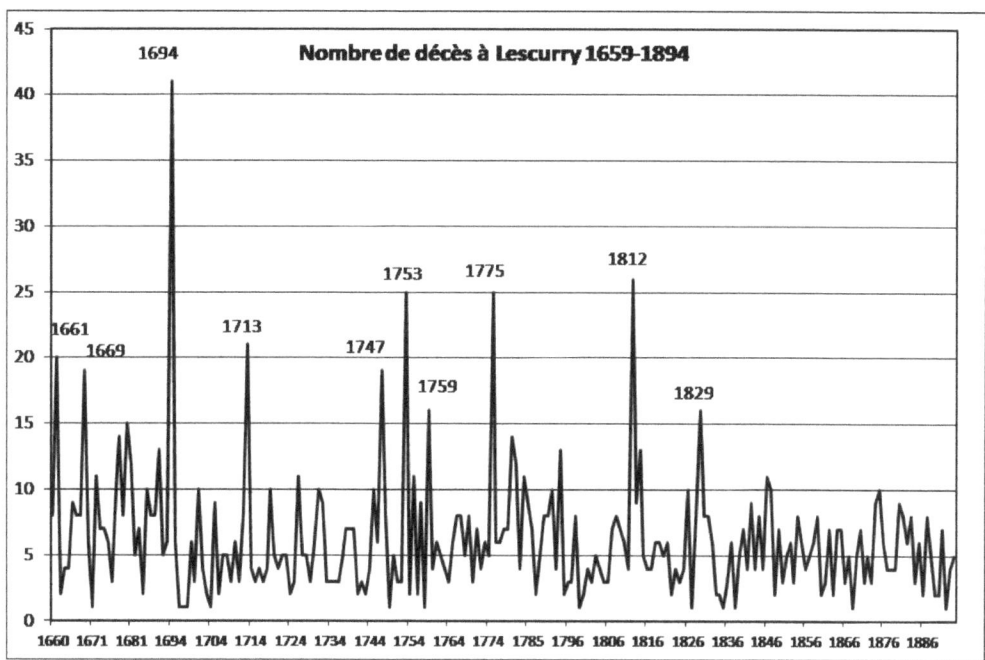

In the autumn of 1713 Lescurry was affected by a significant mortality, perhaps due to famine, but also to the abundant rainfall that occurred that year in the west of France, rainfall which, at that time, could lead to epidemics following the contamination of the water.

But the year 1714 marked the beginning of a new growth that resulted in an improvement in the birth rate.

And then, again in 1747 and 1753, Lescurry was again not spared. In the South-West, after a disturbed and rainy spring, the summer of 1751 experienced an extraordinary drought, with great heat that caused the harvest to perish. There is a lack of grassland. It was a most critical and scarcity year which seems to have resulted in a peak in mortality at Lescurry some time later in 1753.

Regarding the years 1750 and in particular 1751 to 1756, the historian Emmanuel Le Roy Ladurie indicates that they correspond, for France and England, to a series of late years, cold summers and poor harvests. [20]

---

20 Emmanuel Le Roy Ladurie, "Human and Comparative History of the Climate 1740-1860", Fayard.

The harshness of the winters of 1775 and 1794 and the resulting poor harvest led to famine and significant mortality in Lescurry. These successive hecatombs deprived the village of the manpower it needed.

From May to September 1812, mortality was high in Lescurry.

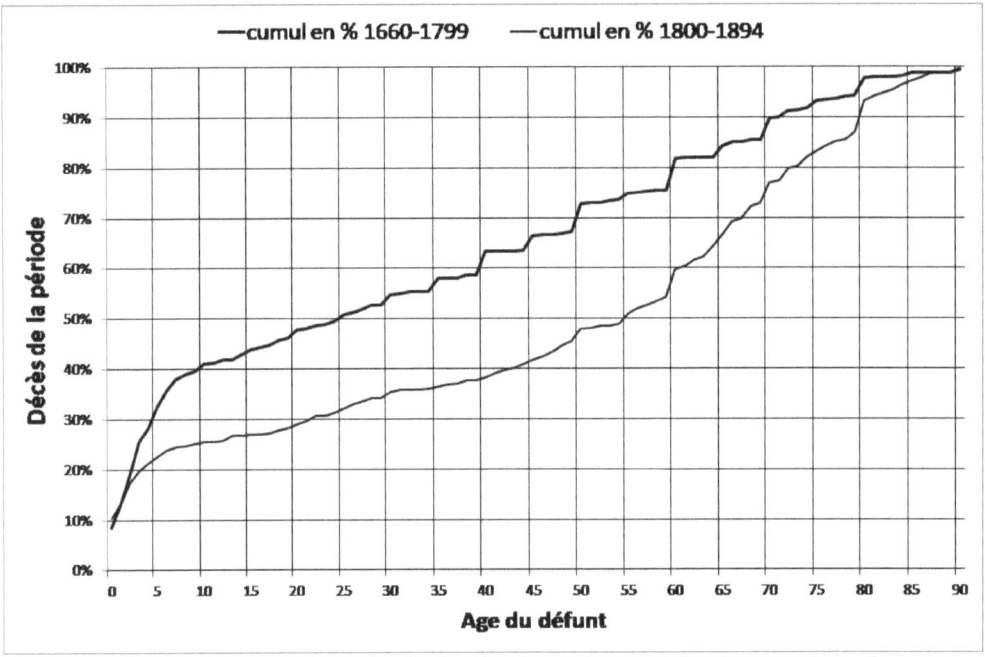

The year 1829 also saw important deaths in autumn. The low water of summer favoring water pollution can explain this mortality once again.

Life expectancy

The age at death mentioned on 74% of the records allows us to draw the graphs opposite which show that for the period 1660-1799, 40% did not exceed the age of 10. However, this percentage fell to 25% for the period 1800-1894.

The graph represents the cumulative deaths observed by age group for the period, expressed as a percentage of total deaths for the period. For example, the 30%, 5-year point of the bold curve means that deaths at ages less than or equal to 5 years, i.e. less than 6 years, represent 30% of the total deaths of the period.

The average age at death presented in the second graph is calculated per 25-year period to account for the small statistical sample size.

These two graphs show the harshness of peasant life until the French Revolution. They also reflect the progress brought about by the nineteenth century. But these

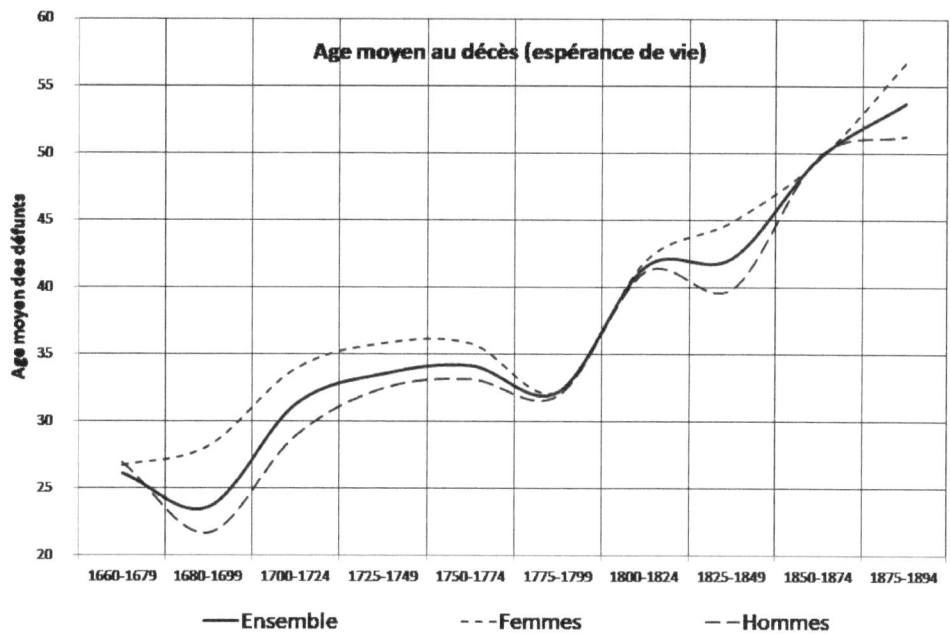

realities are not unique to Lescurry. They have also been observed in other regions of France, notably in Auneuil in Beauvaisis *"between 1657 and 1676 1/3 of the population did not exceed 10 years and 50% did not exceed 20 years of age"* [21]

Women have a higher life expectancy than men. The excess mortality of men at this time was not unique to Lescurry. " *Excess male mortality after the first two years of marriage"* was observed in France in the seventeenth century. The above figures are close to those observed in Auneuil in Beauvaisis: *"21 years under Colbert, 32 years under Necker"* [22]

The cause could be the harshness of the work entrusted to men, which would be a greater factor in mortality than that of mortality in childbirth, in particular.

Births and marriages

In the second half of the seventeenth century, successive famines got the better of the demographic vitality of the village. The average number of births per year has

---

21 Léon, "*Economies et sociétés préindustrielles 1650-1780*". 1970, Armand Collin, p. 51
22 Léon, "*Economies et sociétés préindustrielles 1650-1780*". 1970, Armand Collin, p. 47.

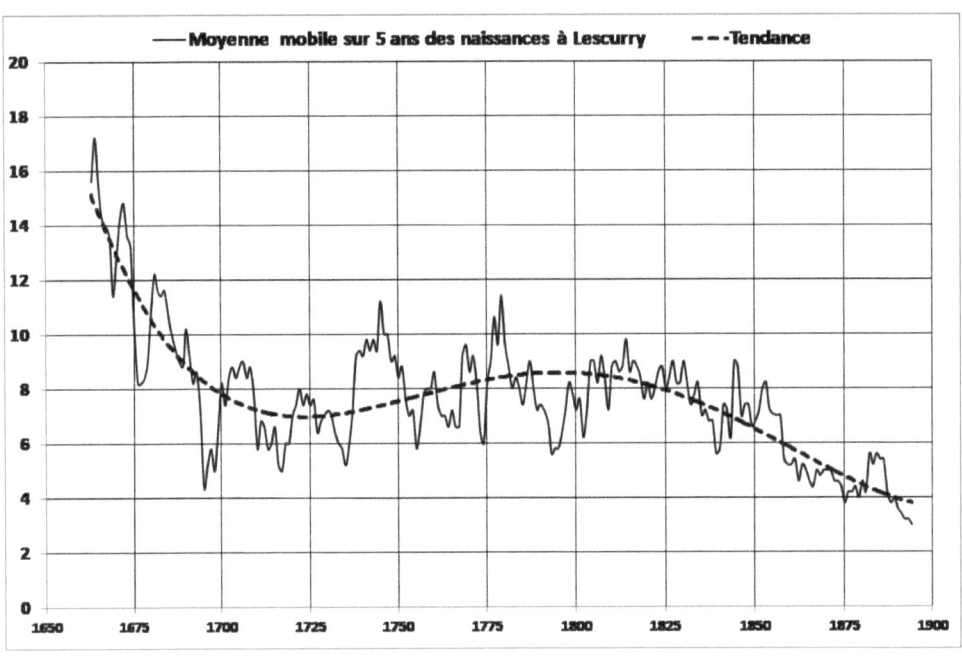

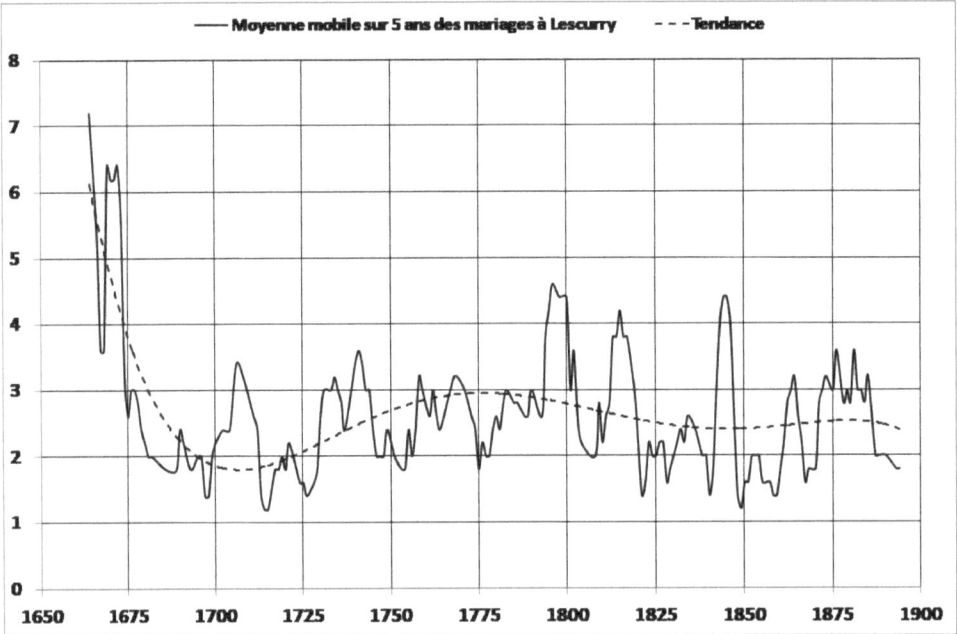

been halved in 50 years. Over the same period, the number of marriages has been divided by three. The demographic vitality observed before the famines of the seventeenth century led to an increase in the number of mouths to feed, which certainly amplified the effect of the famines.

In the eighteenth century, despite the famines that still existed, the number of births increased slightly from 7 births per year to almost 8.5 per year, while the number of marriages increased from two to three

For other reasons due to technical progress, migration and more generally population displacements, the nineteenth century saw a decrease in the annual number of births in Lescurry, which was halved in one century.

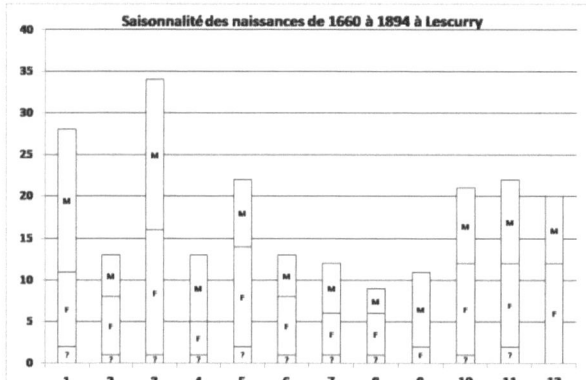

The number of births according to the months of the year varies, but this variation is constant from 1660 to 1894. Over the entire period, the highest number of births was observed in the months of January to March and October to December, and a first decrease in April and May, and finally a more marked decrease between June and September.

The seasonality of births could have a direct link with the mainly agricultural activity of the inhabitants of the village and the marital cult. [23]

The interpretation I propose is that the great physical exertion, due to the hard agricultural work of the months of July and August, prolonged by the no less severe work at that time of year of preparing the soil from September to December, would lead to a decrease in births from April to August. From the middle of the seventeenth century to the end of the nineteenth century, agricultural work was hard and physically exhausted the peasants. This is what this statistic on the seasonality of births seems to tell us.

Life in Lescurry from the middle of the seventeenth century to the end of the eighteenth century

It appears that, from the middle of the seventeenth century to the end of the eighteenth century, life in the village of Lescurry was harsh. Famines, famines,

---

23 The month of May dedicated to the Virgin Mary since 1724, and August 15, a national holiday since 1638, would lead to a decrease and an increase in conceptions in May and August, respectively.

epidemics transformed life into a fight against death. The death of young children inexorably hit all families. You have to feed yourself to survive. To feed oneself one must work hard, but one must also have favourable climatic conditions. In this respect, Lescurry is in line with the national average as described by several historians.

But a favourable evolution was noted during the eighteenth century between 1725 and 1775. Lescurry thus seems to have participated in *"this slow rise in affluence in a part of the rural world"* of which Pierre Goubert speaks for the period of the reign of Louis XV, a statement nuanced by the historian: *"It is advisable, however, not to exaggerate this impression of growing affluence (which some historians deny, without decisive proof)"* [24] Indeed, we can only observe a slight improvement in Lescurry.

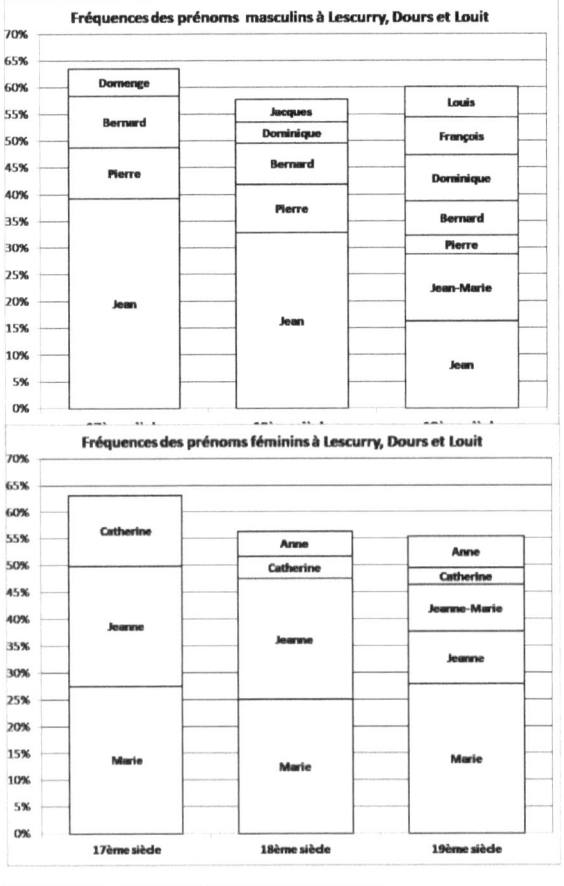

Frequency of first names

The systematic surveys of the parish and civil status registers of Lescurry, Louit and Dours, which I carried out in partnership with other volunteer genealogists, cover 2,789 baptisms and births. The periods concerned are for Lescurry from 1650 to 1894, for Dours from 1680 to 1793, and for Louit from 1647 to 1757. The following statistics therefore concern, for the nineteenth century, exclusively the commune of Lescurry, and for the seventeenth and eighteenth centuries, the three parishes of Lescurry, Dours and Louit.

---

24 Goubert, "Initiation à l'histoire de France", 1984, p. 216.

5. From 1750 to 1800 working to survive

The Cestia of Lescurry, the village of the Cestia

The number of Cestia in the period 1750-1800 is, in Lescurry, about 25 inhabitants, which represents about 10% of the population of the village. Suffice to say that Lescurry is the village of the Cestia.

In the period 1750-1800, despite a number of births that remained stable at about 8 births per year, the population of Lescurry remained stable at about 260 inhabitants. The number of Cestia remained stable over the period, following the demographic evolution of the entire village.

The number of births among the Cestia over the period (0.9 births/year) represents about 10% of the births in the village (8 births/year). These fertility rates should have led to an increase in both the number of inhabitants and the number of Cestia. But the departures to other villages and the mortality due to the famines and epidemics of 1753, 1775 and 1794, prevented population growth. While the average number of deaths in Cestia over the period is 1 death per year, there were 4 deaths in Cestia in 1753 and 2 in 1775 and 1794.

House of Lescurry

In the eighteenth century, Lescurry recorded an average of 6.1 deaths per year. In 1753 there were 25 deaths, 9 of which were in May, in 1775, probably an epidemic [25], caused 25 deaths, 7 of which were in October, in 1794, there were 13 deaths, 7 of which were between April and July.

Departures to other towns or villages were made, in the second half of the eighteenth century, to Dours, Vic-en-Bigorre, Lacassagne, Beccas, Sénac and Bayonne. In total, there are 8 departures from Lescurry between 1750 and 1800. These are young people who settle elsewhere to start a family.

---

25 Famines cause deaths at the time of the lean season between April and July, a large number of deaths in October is more reminiscent of an epidemic.

Life, a fight against death

In the eighteenth century, life was harsh and mortality up to the age of 25 was high. The proportion of an age group over 10 years is only 60% and only 50% reaches the age of 25.

For the Cestia de Lescurry, as in many villages in France, famines, famines and epidemics transformed life into a fight against death. The death of young children, inexorably, hits all families. You have to feed yourself to survive. To feed oneself one must work hard, but the climatic conditions must also be favourable. Equations that are often impossible to solve.

Cestian and Sestian

The Cestia family that can be found in Lescurry between 1750 and 1800 belonged to 19 families (in the sense of the family unit father, mother and children). This includes families where at least one member lived in this period, or only experienced the very beginning of the period, or only the end. These are the Cestian (13 families) or Sestian (5 families) families, but also a Sestiaa family.

The presence in Lescurry of a Sestiaa family is surprising, since this way of writing the family name with a doubling of the final consonant is not the local custom. But the presence of a Sestiaa in Lescurry can be explained: *"Sestiaa"* is Jean, son of Pierre Jean Sestian of a family of Lescurry. Pierre Jean Sestian, the father, married and settled in Nay where his 11 children were called Sestiaa as was customary in Nay. Then one of his eleven children, Jean Sestiaa the son, married in Nay where he had 3 children named Sestiaa. It was then that he moved to Lescurry with his wife and three children. In Lescurry he has 11 more children who bear the name of Sestia.

Apart from this exception of migration from Nay to Lescurry, the Cestian and Sestian de Lescurry in the period 1750-1800 all originated from the village of Lescurry.

We are used to a flawless transmission of the family name today. This was not the case in the eighteenth and nineteenth centuries. We see that a simple change of region leads to the replacement of the ending *"an"* by the ending *"aa"*, then another move just in the other direction allows a "a" to be removed from the ending.

In this period we can observe many cases where the ending in "an" of Cestian or Sestian is not carried over to the next generation, which gives Cestia or Sestia. As for the initial S, it is often replaced from one generation to the next by a C.

The Coubé, Coutillou, Dutrey, Bicata and Bourdale

But who are the Coubé, Coutillou, Dutrey, Bicata and Bourdale de Lescurry? Lescurry is often given a nickname to the Cestian and Sestian de Lescurry, as is customary in Bigorre. The nicknames of the Cestia in Lescurry in the period 1750-1800 are Coubé, Coutillou, Dutrey, Bicata, Biuatou and Bourdale.

The nickname, linked to a house name, is almost as important as the family name since it appears after the family name on the parish registers that record baptisms, marriages and deaths. It is most often awarded at the baptismal certificate. I have also been able to observe in baptismal certificates, in municipal deliberations or private correspondence, that the nickname can exceptionally replace the family name. Its transmission is not hereditary, as it is rare for it to be attributed to an entire sibling. It is not uncommon for first cousins to have the same nickname when they do not have the same surname. As with a family name, the way of writing a nickname is subject to the alteration of time.

The Coubé

The Coubé de Lescurry family in the second half of the eighteenth century were children of the Guillaume brothers and Bernard Cestian.

- Guillaume Cestian a with Marie Sentubery three children who were in this period of the Coubés, Jeanne-Marie (1746-1784), Jeanne (1748-1781) and Jean (1763-1810).
- Jeanne Cestia is the daughter of Bernard Cestian and Gabrielle Bernis. She is a Coubé.

In addition, Guillaume and Bernard Cestian have two nephews Pierre and Jean Sestian whose children are also Coubé. They are Bernard Cestian (1760-1854) and Jeanne Cestia (1768-1777).

The Coutillou

The Coutillou de Lescurry of the same period are Jean, Rose and Jeanne, three children of Guillaume Cestian Coutillou-Darric (1731-1790) and Marthe Dumestre. We also meet another Coutillou in this period, Jean Cestian (1745-1815) Dutrey-Coutillou, first cousin of Guillaume Cestian Coutillou-Darric.

The Dutrey

The Dutrey de Lescurry, also in the same period, were children of the brothers Jean Cestian Dutrey-Coutillou (1745-1815) and Raymond Cestia (1747-1796).

- Jean Cestian Dutrey-Coutillou and Bernarde Darric had three children who were called Dutrey.
- Raymond Cestia has a son, Thomas, also known as Dutrey.
- A first cousin of Jean Cestian and Raymond Cestia, Jean Cestian is also known as Dutrey-Coutillou.

Bicata and Biuatou

The Bicata and Biuatou de Lescurry were children and grandchildren of Jean Cestian Bicata (1667-1731). But his son Bernard Cestian (1692-1781) bears the nickname of Saucetter which comes from his wife from Dours and the Sauceter house in Dours.

Of the children of Jean Cestian Bicata's first marriage to Bernarde Gardey, Bernard is the only one to have a nickname.

The children of Jean Cestian Bicata's second marriage to Catherine Louise Clemens, are Marie Cestian (1697-1762)), Arnauld Cestian Castatou (1716-1788) and Claire Cestian Casta (1718-1761). Marie Cestian has no nickname. It is therefore possible that his parents' house changed after he was born.

In the next generation, Jean Cestian Bicata's grandchildren are Cestian Bicatan (1743-1743), Clear Cestian Biuatou (1744-1744), Etienne Cestian Biuatou (1748-1783)Mary Cestian Biccatan (1751-1753)Anne Cestian Biccatan (1756-1756).

The Bourdale

During the period 1750-1800, the Bourdale de Lescurry family was Bernard Cestian Bourdale (1720-1781) and two of his 6 children Marie (1750-1826) and another of his daughters also named Marie (1751-1801).

The notables of Lescurry

In the eighteenth century, most of the population could not read, write, or even sign their name, except for the nobles and a few rare people. The same was true in Lescurry, where only the nobles who lived in the castle and a few rare people, especially those who were part of the municipal body (municipal council) or who held office, such as that of tax collector, could write and sign their names. Tax collector, an eternal profession, already mentioned in the bible... Under the Ancien Régime, royal taxes were very numerous. These taxes were in addition to the taxes paid to the seigneurs and the Catholic clergy.

In 1768, it was Arnauld Cestian Biuatou (1716-1788) who has this responsibility. He had 9 children between 1736 and 1748, of whom only 3 survived at the time he took office.

Through this example, we can see that mortality can affect everyone, even those who benefit from more education and therefore undoubtedly better living conditions.

Complaints and reprimands from the community of Lescurry

Book of grievances

In order to prepare the States-General, each town and village drew up a collection of complaints and legislative proposals. These collections are then the subject of successive summaries by administrative level which culminate in a final synthesis submitted to the king

Taxes are as old as the world, and so is their unpopularity... Thus, in March 1789 in Lescurry, a list of grievances was drawn up with a view to the preparation of the Estates-General. Tax protests feature prominently. This document signed by nine members of the municipal body, including Jean Cestia, known as Dutrey-Coutillou also demands more justice, equality before taxation *"in proportion to the properties and faculties of each".*

The inhabitants, through the intermediary of the municipal body, demanded "to be free and freed from all degrading and tyrannical yokes", they wanted the "return of freedom which will always be the soul of all commerce". If they did not wish to pay for the "repair of churches and the subsistence of the poor", they nevertheless wanted respect for the "residence of the bishops in each diocese". Surprisingly, this text seems not to have aged...

Book of Grievances, Complaints and Remonstrances to be Formed by the Community of Lescurry

The text below is the transcription in current French of a text whose turns of phrase and words sometimes borrow from old French.

1. That all royal impositions and public charges whatsoever be generally and indiscriminately borne by all orders of citizens in proportion to the property and faculties of each.
2. The periodic return of the holding of the Estates-General and the granting of taxes only after they have been held and on condition that an exact detailed knowledge of the reality is taken in order to proportionate the sacrifice of the subjects.
3. A new constitution of the states of the province, based on the principle of that of the Dauphiné, in which the communities of the countryside have a just representation.
4. An opinion [right to vote] per capita in both the Estates General and the provinces.
5. That the Third Estate be allowed to choose freely and exclusively its syndic and [its] governors with the other orders, a receiver or treasurer, at a discount or by subscription [negotiator or subject to the lump sum] by giving a sufficient guarantee.
6. The abolition of private stallions because they are onerous and contrary to the purpose of their establishment, because private individuals are not free to choose the destination of their mare, which the inspector disposes of at his whim (which is an attack on the right of property), they become disgusted with this branch of economy, which results in a striking reduction in the

number of horses, which will never be remedied except by the return of freedom, which will always be the soul of the any trade.

7. The abolition of the militia in the countryside, so detrimental to tranquillity and so fatal to the repose of families, and to let them subsist in the towns.
8. The abolition of the seigniorial quaestors as a most onerous office and are a degree of jurisdiction which only procures more expense. To regulate justice by two degrees of jurisdiction, the first deferred up to two hundred livres, to the seneschal two thousand livres, to the presidial four thousand livres, and to the rest to the parliament as a final report, that all proceedings end within the year of the proceedings.
9. Abolition of seigneurial corvées and other personal rights which, like the remains of servitude, essentially wound the dignity of man and annihilate the most precious and dear prerogative of the French, which is to be free and free from all degrading and tyrannical yokes.
10. The suppression of the *"banality"* [26] of the mills as one of the most odious rights of feudalism which serves only to promote, even to protect a brigandage all the more deplorable because it is exercised mainly on the most indigent part of the people, who are obliged to grind their grain in very small detail [quantity], because it is only the product of their wages or their industry, is exposed to more repeated losses and all the more constant because its weakness ensures impunity. It is for this reason that the mills are satisfied [27] although they are commonly leased at an exorbitant price: the millers, by their fatal skill which they put into their means of exercising [their] rapacity, always find there something to pay and often something to enrich themselves.
11. The abolition of the right of pre-emption [28] as extremely harmful to the interests of families, to the good of the farmer, to the freedom of trade to the interests of families, because the present circumstances require, especially in calamitous years, temporary assistance requiring the sale of objects at a low price in order to take them back in the course of the year, but of which they are deprived by the exercise of the right of pre-emption, so likely to

---

26 In the French feudal system, banalities were technical installations that the lord was obliged to maintain and make available to any inhabitant of the seigneury. In return, the inhabitants of this seigneury could only use these seigneurial facilities for a fee.

27 The text uses the word *"ebanier"*, a word from the Old French *"Esbanoier"*, to rejoice, to entertain, to cheer up, according to the Godefroy Dictionary.

28 The text uses the word *"prelation"* which in feudal times refers to the right of pre-emption or right of retention in prelation.

encourage a shameful and unjust traffic, by lucrative resales or by transfer in favour of the protégés to the property of the farmer, because the purchasers cannot count on their acquisition, of which many lords refuse for several years to give them the investiture and neglect the improvements they would be liable to the freedom of trade, because the By keeping competition away, it is harmful to the seller, as well as to households who would like to seize the opportunity to invest the fruit of their savings in the objects of their convenience if seigniorial privileges did not often hinder it.

12. That the communities be authorized to appoint their consuls themselves, either because it is not proper for the lords to appoint the administrators of a country with which they often have opposing interests, or because it is indecent, in cases where the lords do not reside, that the appointments should be made by servants or their agents who are not competent to judge the merits of the subjects.
13. The restitution of the portion of the tithes consecrated by the ancient canons and ordinances of the kingdom to the repair of the churches and the subsistence of the poor.
14. The destitution of the *"masters"* [29] who only served to protect the lords and the ruin of the subjects by the injustice that was exercised in practice.
15. The abolition of the right to hunt and fish on all public rivers as being harmful to the common people. The lords having the authority of right to appropriate fines against their vassals and others who would have the weakness to concern themselves with the said ministry, a single moment on the part of the said lords surprised ensued.
16. The abolition of pontoonage and tolls, that passengers be free on the bridges that are found in all kinds of roads.
17. The suppression of the tenth, considering that the cathedral of the diocese of Tarbes has rents of seven to eight thousand livres, that the towns of which it holds the tenth do not have enough rents to maintain themselves, and that if they have a title of possession, it is only by virtue that when the cathedral of the diocese was burned, The chapter asked for the tenth for the rebuilding of the choir for a certain time and they have unscrupulously continued the process until today.

---

29 Controls: these are administrative authorisations for certain activities, for example "water and forest control".

18. That the high clergy, abbots, and community of the priory, and annuitants be subject and taxpayers to the payment of the royal debts on the tenth of their rents.
19. The residence of the bishops in each diocese since the absence of bishops is very prejudicial to the subjects to take orders, and very expensive to transport themselves to foreign dioceses to succeed in taking holy orders.
20. The abolition of the "vaquat" [30] which is paid in the two dioceses of Tarbes and Léseas alone of half of the usufruct of the year of the death of the parish priest who dies, without regard under any circumstances whether there is hail or other plagues that may have occurred.
21. The suppression of tithes on lambs, birds and other species of " *carnalage*" [31right].
22. Let all kinds of characters be subject to general chores or taxes for the maintenance of roads.
23. That under no pretext, nor for any reason whatsoever, may the ministers, the tribunals, or any subject of the king violate the laws with impunity.
24. To suppress the special donations which are made to the states of the province in Bigorre to the prejudice of the public only in cases of fire or other scourges worthy of the merit of charity.
25. That all the king's subjects without distinction contribute to the payment of the debt of the State, that the lords of the land and all the possessors of privileged and non-privileged noble property be subject to the amount of the national debt.
26. That the bailiffs be taxed at the same place for the distance from which the said bailiffs take their commission.
27. That it be permitted to any owner to take away and remove his crop as soon as he has gathered it, and leave the portion of the tithe in the said room, without being obliged to wait for the will of the decimator, since frequent plagues may occur there, or other accidents.
28. The commune particularly states that the lord of the place owns about five hundred and seventy-two forest logs in the place with a noble title, it is requested that the lord be subject and by subscription [forfait] to the royal taxes included in the rolls of the said place.

---

30 Vaque, adj., unoccupied for a function.

31 Carnalage, subst. masc, (Southern Provinces) Right of carnalage. "Right to seize cattle caught in places where it is forbidden to graze" Middle French Dictionary, 2015, Robert Martin.

29. The said lord having invested himself or its authors [responsible] with one hundred journals of land consisting of woods and moors by his private authority, if titles do not follow, the funds belonging to the said community entirely after the enumeration of 1614 following the last regulation of the States-General in France, that the lords be subject to the abandonment of the land in favor of the inhabitants as usurped to their prejudice, or that the lord be ordered to justify the acquisition of the said land by providing just and non-disputable titles before the Seneschal of Tarbes to be said to be entitled to it
30. Finally, the inhabitants asked to be kept under the law of enumeration of 1614 to pay the seigneurial dues.
31. The suppression of all tenders concerning couriers, which have an exclusive right to any other inhabitant of the kingdom to take charge of all travellers, and make any other carrier who earns his living pay unduly three livres per seat, which goes against French liberty and against natural law and civil and

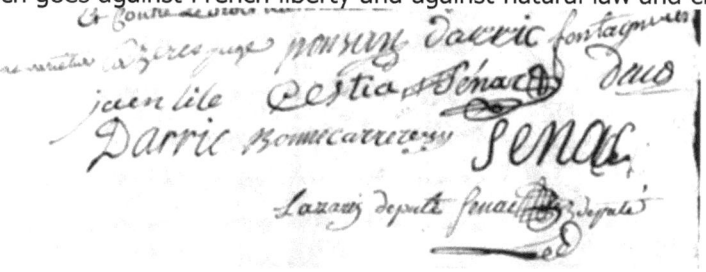

national law.

Lescurry, March 28, 1789

Among the signatories, members of the municipal body, was Jean Cestia Dutrey-Coutillou (1745-1815) and Bernard Duco First Consul, husband of Jeanne Marie Cestian (1745-1794) the daughter of the late Guillaume Cestia dit Coubé tax collector.

1790, the year of the tax adjustment

Well, do we get it right... in Lescurry in 1790, the tax adjustment concerned the tax collectors of the Ancien Régime... and not the adjustment of taxpayers. Lescurry was far from Versailles and Paris, but the Third Estate, which proclaimed itself a national assembly - the Bastille stormed by rioters, and on August 26, 1789 - the Declaration of the Rights of Man and of the Citizen, stirred up the village.

Thus, according to the municipal deliberation, on September 7, 1790 in Lescurry, and where the commune is customary to hold its assemblies, the mayor and municipal officers with his council, here present, proceeded to the verification of the accounts to be rendered by the collectors, on the basis of the Royal Moneys which consist of size, twentieth, triple twentieth, in order to know the receipts and expenses, and in order to be reimbursed by the collectors, in favor of the community of the sums that may be due to it, from the most taxed on the rolls, to be remitted to the collectors, from the least taxed and begin from the year 1761 to including the year 1789"

So on that day, the 10 tax collectors who had officiated from 1761 to 1789 were there, or were represented by their heirs, to present the accounts relating to their office.

The first presents his accounts and reimburses 3 livres 15 sous, then the following reimburse each a few sous and a few deniers.

"Then came Mr. Jacques Frechou Bicata, representing Arnauld Cestia collector of the year 1768, who after having rendered his account found himself in debt of 3 sous, 9 deniers which he paid and handed over to the municipal officers"

Tax collector Arnauld Cestia Biuata died in May 1788 at the age of 71. None of his children survives him. In 1790 his only descendants were Jean Lalanne de Dours a 10-year-old grandson and Jeanne Cestia a 14-year-old granddaughter of Lescurry. No one in his descendants can therefore represent him. Jacques Frechou was therefore chosen the second husband of Jacquette Darieux, whose first husband was Etienne Cestian dit Biuata (1748-1783), the son of the tax collector. Jacques Fréchou therefore presented the accounts of his wife's father-in-law and paid, 22 years later, the family debt of 3 sous ... for the financial year of 1768.

Then Darric and Duco arrive, to whom 6 sous and 6 deniers and 16 sous 4 deniers are reimbursed with due justification. (At that time a day's work was worth about 26 cents).

And it is then the turn to examine the accounts of the said Coubé collector for the years 1763, 1764, 1765, 1778, 1779 and 1780. It is his son who represents him and *"who, after having rendered his account, found himself in debt for 18 livres, 1 denarius that remains to be paid..."* (1 Livre tournois = 20 sous = 240 deniers)

This session of 7 September 1790 made it possible to examine the accounts of 29 years of tax collection, with the exception of the years 1726 and 1775. The year 1726, perhaps because of an important tax reform whose texts arrived late and did not allow the tax to be collected, and the year 1775, perhaps because of the famine that raged that year.

In total, the collection of this tax adjustment is 34 livres 6 sous 8 deniers, i.e. the equivalent in wages for 26 days. ... Good accounts make good friends, in Lescurry in 1790, democracy not yet proclaimed, is on the right track!

The Cestia de Nay

In the nineteenth century, the Cestia de Nay family was a large family that worked in the textile and wood industries. In 1750, there were families in Nay who had been there for several generations. This is the descendant of the family of Sestiaa Jean married Laffont, hosiery. Her first children bear the name Sestiaa, while the next ones are Sestia.

There are also families who have their origins in Lescurry or whose parents from Lescurry married in Nay and settled there at the beginning of the century. They are the children of Pierre Jean Sestian dit Dauveille de Lescurry who married Anne Pehourtic in Nay with whom he had 12 children born between 1696 and 1720, of whom only 6 reached adulthood. They are also the children of Jean Sestian merchant who had, with Jeanne Margueritte Anne Gouailles, 11 children between 1702 and 1738, of whom only 4 reached adulthood. From Lescurry there are also those who came from Lescurry with their wives and children like Bernard and Jean Sestian.

Thus the Cestia, Sestian, Sestia and Sestiaa who lived between 1750 and 1800 in Nay, have close family ties.

The Cestia de Nay married in their town and usually had at least 5 children there. Between 1750 and 1800, the number of Cestia increased in Nay by about 45%. They kept their parents' trade and contrary to what we saw in Bigorre in the nineteenth century, they did not seek their fortune elsewhere, they stayed in their industrial town which provided them with work and wages.

Apart from the few shopkeepers and craftsmen, who were bakers, shoemakers, innkeepers or stonemasons, the other Cestia were most often workers in the wool industry (laneficier), knitters or weavers. Half of them work in the textile industry, particularly the wool industry, but 20% have a job in the wood industry.

In Nay there is in the city center the royal factory of Turkish caps, created by the Poey brothers of Oloron around 1740. This factory produced woollen headdresses that were exported to the Orient and the Mediterranean region. There are also older factories near the waterways specializing in the manufacture of woollen blankets and cadis (large bure fabrics). In Nay, the river Gave de Pau provided the water necessary for these pre-industrial factories in Nay, which in the eighteenth century attracted populations from all over Bigorre and the Cestia de Lescurry in particular.

The Cestia de Nay, many of whom were workers in the factories, had difficult living conditions. This did not cause them to leave because they were more numerous in the nineteenth century than they were in the eighteenth century. But this attachment to their city, which is perpetuated from generation to generation, is paradoxical in the context of their working condition. It would be risky to conclude that they are satisfied with their lot. Is this situation the result of a trade-off between the condition of peasant and that of worker, or the result of an impossible choice? Did the Cestia de Nay prefer to be a worker for a salary that barely allows them to survive, earlier than to work the land for a meagre profit and sometimes for nothing when the climate is not favorable?

The Cestia were employees of these factories *"subsisting, from day to day, on a meagre salary, legally free, but economically dependent?"* as Pierre Léon, historian and professor at the University of Lyon, wonders about the factories of Lyon. [32].

The answer to these questions may be found in this extract from the *"Mémoire sur les manufactures de Lyon"* addressed to the King in 1786 by Etienne Mayet, Director of the King's Factories of Prussia and Assessor at the Royal Chamber of Manufactures.

The dissertation below concerns Lyon. It seems to me, however, that it also applies to the royal manufactory of Nay, whose creation predates that of Lyon.

> "To ensure and maintain the prosperity of our manufactures, it is necessary that the worker never get richer, that he has precisely what he needs to feed and clothe himself well. In a certain class of the people, too much affluence softens industry, engenders idleness and all the vices that depend on it. In proportion as the worker becomes richer, he becomes difficult about the choice and the wages of labor. Once the wage of the workforce has been increased, it increases because of the advantages it provides. It's a torrent that has broken … Everyone knows that it is mainly to the low price of labour that the factories of Lyon owe their astonishing prosperity. If necessity ceases to compel the workman to receive from the occupation whatever wages are offered to him, if he succeeds in freeing himself from this kind of servitude, if his profits exceed his needs to such an extent that he can subsist for some time without the help of his hands, he will employ this time in forming a league. Not ignorant that the merchant cannot eternally do without him, he will, in his turn, dare to prescribe to him the laws which will put the latter out of a position to withstand any competition with foreign manufactures, and from this reversal, to which the well-being of the worker will have given rise, will come the total ruin of the factory. It is therefore very important for the manufacturers of Lyons to keep the worker in a continual need of work, never to forget that the low price of labor is not only advantageous to them in itself, but that it becomes so even more so by making the worker more laborious, more regulated in his morals, more submissive to their wills. »

The Cestia de Louit

In the second half of the eighteenth century, the village of Louit was poor. We haven't yet gone to Guadeloupe or Puerto Rico to make a fortune and bring back a little comfort and wealth from the islands. But the situation in Louit is certainly not as bad as that of the neighbouring village, Lescurry. This is what we feel about the fact that two Cestia families left Lescurry during this period to settle in Louit.

Lescurry is only a few kilometres north of Louit, about 1 hour walk. This is how Jean and Jean Cestian two brothers born in Lescurry in 1699 and 1708 married in Louit.

---

32 Pierre Léon, "Economies et sociétés préindustrielles 1650-1780", 1970, Armand Colin, page 375.

One married Marguerite Guinle and the other Marie Luit. Their wives were born in Louit.

It is no longer customary today to give the same first name to two of your children. In the eighteenth century, it was quite frequent. I don't know why. But given the infant mortality, perhaps it is to be sure of having at least one surviving child of the name we hold dear, often that of the father. Pure hypothesis on my part.

In the two families from Lescurry who settled in Louit, the father was also called Jean... That's a lot of Jean. But in the eighteenth century this name was very fashionable; it is given in the Cestia families in 35% of baptisms, ahead of Bernard 16% and Pierre 10%. For girls, Jeanne is almost equal with Marie with 29% and 28% of baptisms respectively, followed by Anne at 11%. (See "Frequency of first names» page 38)

The two Jean Cestians, one known as Guillaumet and the other known as Guilhem, born in Lescurry, settled in Louit between 1735 and 1740. They were the first bearers of this surname in Louit.

Of the marriage of Jean Cestian dit Guillaumet with Marguerite Guinle Pierre was born in 1736, Françoise in 1738, Bernard in 1741 and Guillaume in 1744. Françoise married Bernard Dupont, Bernard died in the year of his birth and Guillaume settled in Vic-en-Bigorre around 1760.

Of the marriage of Jean Cestian dit Guilhem with Marie Luit two daughters were born in 1737 and 1742. In 1742, Marie Luit, who had become a widow, married to Louit Guilhaume Cestian Lescurry brewer with whom she had a daughter and a son with whom no descendants are known.

The Cestia de Dours

In 1800, the village of Dours had about 150 inhabitants. The territory of the commune of Dours adjoins that of Louit.

In 1750, in Dours, there were the 4 children of Arnaud Sestian of Dours dit Saucetter and Marie Adamet his wife. Their children were born in Dours between 1732 and 1745. Two of the four children were recorded in the parish registers under the name of Sextia by a parish priest who was acting for the former parish priest who had just died. Why this replacement of the s by an x. Sestius is a Roman given name while Sextius is a Roman given name. This priest must have been more cultured than the previous one...

Then, in the next generation, Bernard, one of Arnaud and Marie's children born in Dours, had in 1760 in Dours with Marie Lamon a daughter Jeanne. On the other hand, Bernard's brother married and settled in Lansac where he had 4 children.

There is also in Dours Jacques the brother of Arnaud who has 7 children with Anne St Ubery between 1809 and 1826

Between 1750 and 1800, Dours, like Louit, continued to attract Cestia de Lescurry who found in this small village more generous land than that of Lescurry. They thus join the Cestia already present in Dours. Thus Bernard Cestian Saucetter, originally from Lescurry, settled and married in Dours with Domengea Père and then with Anne St Upery his second wife.

Vic-en-Bigorre

Antoine Cestia born in Vic-en-Bigorre to a family originally from Louit a, in Vic, with Anne Bire 2 children born between 1786 and 1789.

Buzon

Jeanne Marie Cestian de Beccas marries Buzon

Lansac

In Lansac were born the 4 children of Jean Cestian dit Sausette from Dours and his wife Jeannette Louit

Sénac

In Sénac, Jean Cestian Coubé's 4 children were born of Lescurry and Marguerite Cougot

6. Slavery in France in the nineteenth century

Slavery was the only mode of production in the West Indies from 1680 to 1848. Until the middle of the nineteenth century, the sugar industry in Guadeloupe was very little mechanized. It then experienced a very strong growth which made the constant lack of slaves since the beginning of the slavery period all the more noticeable. Until 1831, the French slave trade, which had been banned since 1814, continued almost openly thanks to the passive complicity of the authorities. It was in 1832 that the slave population of Guadeloupe reached its peak: there were nearly 100,000 slaves who represented 80% of the total population of the island. The effective end of the slave trade and the implementation by the July Monarchy of a policy facilitating emancipation led to a decrease in the servile population. [33].

"But the horror remains, because slavery itself remains," writes the historian Schnakenburg [34] which continues, "The comparison often made by apologists for slavery under the July Monarchy between the situation of the slave and the proletarian is meaningless", it is for me above all amoral. In law as in fact, slaves are not persons" see "Code noir promulgated in March 1685 by Louis XIV» page 54

In the middle of the nineteenth century, the anti-slavery struggle became more and more economic and was based less and less on moral and humanitarian arguments. For the Classics, the economists who inspired the liberal reforms under the July Monarchy, slavery was not profitable enough. It must therefore be abolished. [35]. From 1830 onwards, these arguments began to bear fruit, particularly in public opinion, but in practice only led to the decision to effectively stop the slave trade. During this same period, acts of resistance by slaves multiplied in the West Indies, except in Guadeloupe, where the harsh repression of the uprisings of 1802 seems to have prevented other attempts at revolt.

In the middle of the nineteenth century, uncertainty about the future of the slave system plunged the economy of Guadeloupe into serious difficulties. The increase in the price of slaves, due to the effective cessation of the slave trade, led to an increase

---

33 Cf. Christian Schnakenbourg, "The Crisis of the Slave System 1835-1847", Armantan edition.

34 Christian Schnakenbourg holds a doctorate in law and economics. He is an assistant professor at the EBU of Economics and Management at the University of Amiens. He focused his research on the economic history of the West Indies. He has devoted a thesis and numerous articles to this subject.

35 The classics mention the excessive price of slaves, the investment risk that buying a slave represents, the high maintenance costs since the slave must be cared for and fed even in unproductive times, and the low productivity of the slave who has every good reason to do as little as possible.

in production costs. The shock of the sudden decrease in production in Saint-Domingue from 1802 onwards initially favoured production and profits, but then produced a crisis of overproduction from 1830 onwards (cf. Schnakenburg).

Code noir promulgated in March 1685 by Louis XIV

The Black Code of 1685 had 60 articles that set out rights and duties. It is Article 44 that determines the slave's patrimonial situation.

- Article 44 We declare the slaves to be movable and as such to enter into the community, not to have a succession by mortgage, to be divided equally among the co-heirs, without preciput and birthright, not to be subject to customary dower, to feudal and lineage withdrawal, to feudal and seigniorial rights, to the formalities of decrees, nor to the retrenchment of the four quints, in the event of disposition upon death and testamentary. »

But a limit was set: "Husband, wife and their prepubescent children may not be seized and sold separately if they are all under the power of the same master"

These articles were preceded by articles that granted slaves rights.

- Slaves who are not fed, clothed, and maintained by their masters, as we have hereby ordered, may give notice thereof to our attorney general." The master has an obligation to provide for the needs of slaves "crippled by old age, sickness or otherwise

The Black Code imposes the Catholic religion

- All the slaves who shall be in our islands shall be baptized and instructed in the Catholic religion. ». Sunday rest is prescribed; "We forbid them to work or to have their slaves work on the said Sundays and feast days

Article 9 prohibits free unions between masters and slaves but authorizes marriage.

- Article 9 Free men who have had one or more children by their concubinage with slaves, together with the masters who have suffered them, shall each be sentenced to a fine of 2000 pounds of sugar, and, if they are the masters of the slave by whom they have had the said children, we will, in addition to the fine, that they be deprived of the slave and the children and that she and they be tried in the hospital, without ever being able to be freed. However, we do not intend the present article to take place when a free man who was not married to another person during his concubinage with his slave, marries in the forms observed by the Church the said slave, who will be freed by this means and the children made free and legitimate. »

Order and discipline must reign.

- Let us forbid slaves to carry any offensive weapons." No gathering is allowed under any "pretext of marriage or otherwise" the right of property is not granted to slaves: "We declare slaves that they cannot have anything that belongs to their masters."

But Article 32 gives slaves the right to be tried for crimes as free persons.

- Article 32 Slaves may be prosecuted criminally, without the need to make their masters parties, (otherwise) in case of complicity: and accused slaves shall be judged in the first instance by the ordinary judges and by appeal to the Sovereign Council, on the same instruction and with the same formalities as free persons.

However, articles 33 et seq. specify the penalties incurred by slaves, which are most often death.

- Article 33 A slave who strikes his master, mistress, or the husband of his mistress, or their children with bruising or bloodshed, or in the face, shall be punished with death.
- Article 34 And as for the excesses and assaults that shall be committed by slaves against free persons, we want them to be severely punished, even with death, if necessary.
- Article 35 Robberies, even of horses, horses, mules, oxen or cows, which have been committed by slaves or freedmen, shall be punished by afflictive punishments, even by death, if the case so requires.
- Article 36 Thefts of sheep, goats, pigs, poultry, sugar-cane, peas, millet, manioc or other vegetables committed by slaves shall be punished according to the quality of the theft by the judges, who may, if necessary, condemn them to be beaten with rods by the executor of high justice and branded with a fleur-de-lys.

The penalties for fugitives are set out in article 38.

- Article 38 A fugitive slave who has been on the run for a month, from the day on which his master has denounced him in court, shall have his ears cut off and shall be branded with a fleur-de-lis on one shoulder; if he reoffends another month in the same way from the day of the denunciation, he shall have his hock cut off, and he shall be branded with a fleur-de-lis on the other shoulder; and the third time he shall be punished with death.

Masters have the right to inflict corporal punishment,

- *chained and beaten with rods or cords"* but could not *"torture them, nor do they have any mutilation of limbs"* However, the officers could absolve *"without the need for them to obtain from us (the King) letters of pardon*

Chronological landmarks since 1789

From 1789 to 1848, the debate on the abolition of slavery took a long time to culminate in an abolition law in 1848. However, the slave trade was banned in 1815 and became a crime in 1827. For a long time, what was forbidden in metropolitan France was allowed on the islands. It took society as a whole to become aware of his crime.

1789	France – Declaration of the Rights of Man and of the Citizen: *"Men are born free and equal before the law"*
1790	8 March – On the proposal of Barnave, slavery is maintained in the colonies
1790	April 16 – General Assembly of the French part of Santo Domingo
1791	February 25 – In Saint-Domingue, Vincent Ogé and his friend Jean-Baptiste Chavannes suffer the torture of the wheel for opposing slavery
1791	Insurrection of slaves in Saint-Domingue, who obtain the abolition of slavery in the colony on August 29, 1793. Disturbances in Martinique, Guadeloupe
1791	May 15 – A decree maintains slavery
1791	September 24 – Blacks are declared non-citizens
1791	28 September – Slavery is abolished on French soil in mainland France
1792	24 March – Political equality for mulattoes is proclaimed
1793	29 August – Abolition of slavery in Saint-Domingue (Haiti).
1793	September – Called by the colonists, the English land in Saint-Domingue
1794	4 February – Decree of the Convention abolishing slavery in France
1794	Victor Hugues (1761-1826), sent by the French National Convention, governed Guadeloupe. Many guillotines and repressions, dispossessed owners, master of the island he turns out to be venal
1795	22 July – The Spanish part of Santo Domingo returns to Spain
1797	22 August – Toussaint Louverture forces the Commissioner of the Republic to leave Saint-Domingue.
1798	Harassed by Toussaint Louverture, decimated by yellow fever, the English left Saint-Domingue
1801	In Guadeloupe, there was a general revolt after the return of the islands to France, which restored the situation of the Ancien Régime
1802	20 May – Bonaparte re-establishes slavery in the French colonies in accordance with legislation prior to 1789. The large dwellings, for the most part, went to their owners or their descendants, the freedmen who remained on the spot were put back to work with the re-establishment of slavery

1803	7 April – Death of Toussaint Louverture at the Fort de Joux
1804	Proclamation of Haiti's independence
1806	English laws prohibiting the introduction of new slaves into conquered colonies
1807	Prohibition of the slave trade by Great Britain and the importation of captives and slaves by the United States.
1807	Unrest in Martinique
1809	Three cyclones ravaged Guadeloupe in the same year: 27 July, 2 August and 2 September
1814	Despite the Treaties of Paris of 1814 and 1815, which established the supremacy of England, Louis XVIII's France succeeded in recovering Guyana, Martinique, Guadeloupe, Senegal, Reunion, and the trading posts of the Indies. It maintains slavery there. The island of Guadeloupe is taking on the appearance of a sugar colony. It was the beginning of an era of prosperity
1814	Pope Pius VII condemns *"the trade in blacks"* In the past, in 1454, Pope Nicholas V authorized the King of Portugal to practice the slave trade and slavery of Africans. Then in 1537, Pope Julius III condemned any questioning of the full humanity of the Indians
1815	29 March – During the Hundred Days, Napoleon decrees the abolition of the slave trade but not the abolition of slavery
1815	9 June – The European powers commit to banning the slave trade at the Congress of Vienna (Great Britain, France, Austria, Russia, Prussia, Sweden, Portugal)
1815	Continuation of the clandestine trade despite its prohibition.
1817	January 8 – The French government issues an ordinance threatening to confiscate any ship attempting to smuggle blacks into a French colony.
1818	15 April – Louis XVIII prohibits the slave trade within the French colonial empire
1820	Highest point of sugar production in Guadeloupe. There is no talk of the abolition of slavery and there is no perception that the structures are obsolete
1821	Creation in Paris of the Society of Christian Morals and, in 1822, of its Committee for the Abolition of the Slave Trade and Slavery
1824	A cyclone ravages Guadeloupe. Recurrent weather phenomenon in Guadeloupe. In the eighteenth century 15 cyclones were recorded, in the nineteenth century there were 20, in the twentieth century there were 26 (cf. http://www.ouragans.com/)

1827	25 April – Charles X prohibits the slave trade within the French colonial empire. The offence is no longer a misdemeanour but a crime
1830	The last slave ship from Nantes to be recognized as such was Virginia. In Guadeloupe, 602 sugar houses
1830	Schoelcher spoke out against immediate abolition because, for him, *"the negroes, who had come out of the hands of their masters with the ignorance and all the vices of slavery, would be good for nothing, neither for society nor for themselves"*
1831	February 22 – Third French law prohibiting the slave trade. Anglo-French Agreement for the Control of the Illicit Slave Trade
1833	Schoelcher published an indictment against slavery and its abolition, but he referred it to a *"future revolutionary incident that I would like to see with the rest of my wishes"*
1833 1838	Abolition of slavery in the British colonies of the West Indies, British Guiana, Mauritius. The position of the supporters of slavery was weakened in the French West Indies
1834	Creation in Paris of the French Society for the Abolition of Slavery
1839	Creation in London of the British and Foreign Anti-Slavery Society. Pope Gregory XVI officially condemns the slave trade
1840 1842	Victor Schoelcher's second trip to the Caribbean. He advocated abolition. Publication and political action in favour of abolition. He came up against the censal power established in the colonies in 1827 and reformed in 1833. In 1835, for every 12,000 whites, there were 19,000 free people of colour whose power was limited by the censal system. The debate on abolition took place in a climate of economic stagnation in the French colonies. Despite his humanism, Schoeler used economic arguments to defend abolition: the cost of capital tied up and its maintenance was higher than in the wage system. In a context of rising abolitionist ideas, blacks became impatient, strikes multiplied
1843	8 February – Terrible earthquake in Pointe-à-Pitre, causing a large number of victims
1843	Arrival in metropolitan France of new sugar powers with the development of beet sugar. In Guadeloupe, home sales are multiplying. The establishment of cane processing factories deprived the planters of the resources of the sugar industry and at the same time the abolition of the slave trade deprived them of slave labour.

1848	27 April – Victor Schœlcher, appointed by Lamartine as president of the commission for the abolition of slavery, was the initiator of the decree of 27 April 1848 definitively abolishing slavery in France. By this decree, the Second Republic abolished slavery in the colonies
1849	Last suspected French slave ship: the Tourville would have landed slaves in Brazil
1849	30 April – Parliament establishes a system of compensation for all the colonies.
1852	February – First French decrees for the recruitment of free workers on contract in Africa and then in India, for the Caribbean colonies
1861	End of the "colonial exclusivity" [36] put in place from the beginning of colonization to the benefit of the economy of France, despite the constant demand of the colonists for freedom of trade.
1863 1865	The end of the American Civil War led to the federal abolition of slavery in the United States
1866	Spanish Decree Prohibiting the Slave Trade
1870	The economic crisis and cataclysm weakened the colonial sugar industry. Credit agencies recovered the land of indebted settlers. Many people returned to mainland France from this period onwards
1873	Abolition of slavery in the Spanish colony of Puerto Rico

Colonial indemnity in Guadeloupe

The decree of 27 April 1848 abolished slavery in all French colonies and possessions. In its preamble, it proclaims that slavery is an attack on human dignity and a flagrant violation of the republican dogma: Liberty, Equality, Fraternity. This decree also established the principle of indemnity and prudently left it to Parliament to fix the proportion of the indemnity that should be granted to the colonists.

By the law of 30 April 1849, the parliament set a system of compensation for all the colonies consisting of an indemnity of 6 million francs payable immediately and an annual annuity of 6 million francs paid for 20 years, i.e. 120 million francs in total. The parliament thus pursues an objective of both social cohesion and economic balance. For the territories of Guadeloupe, Martinique and Réunion, it required the creation of a loan and discount bank endowed with capital by levying one-eighth of

---

36 The Colonial Exclusivity governed trade between the colonies and France from the sixteenth century onwards. Everything that the colony produced had to be exported to the metropolis and everything that the colony imported had to come from the metropolis or be transported by French ships.

the annuity allocated to owners who had received more than 1,000 francs in compensation. For them, this levy takes the form of shares in the future bank.

The total amounts of compensation set by law are distributed by decree in the various territories concerned: Martinique, Guadeloupe and dependencies, Réunion, French Guiana, Senegal and dependencies, and Nossi-Bé and Sainte-Marie. This distribution was not made in proportion to the number of slaves enumerated in each of the territories, but probably according to the number and market value of the slaves. The allowance represents about 40% of this value.

Guadeloupe obtained 1.95 million francs for each of the indemnities in cash and capital, or 32.5% of the total amount fixed by law, for about one thousand to two thousand *"habitations"* [37] employing 87,087 slaves, or 35.1% of the total number of slaves in all the colonies. Thus, a former owner was compensated for a slave by the immediate payment of 22.35 francs and by an annuity of 20 times 22.35 francs, i.e. a total of 469.35 francs, of which 55.85 francs were paid in shares of the colonial bank of Guadeloupe.

Compensated for the most part in annuities of 20 times 5%, owners may prefer to monetize their annuity securities, rather than receive an annual annuity. Small landowners have significant cash flow needs; They now have to pay salaries and modernize their farms. They are therefore often obliged to negotiate their liquidation certificates. [38]

Memorial Act of 21 May 2001

Act No. 2001-434 of 21 May 2001 on the recognition of the slave trade and slavery as a crime against humanity.

Article 1: The French Republic recognizes that the transatlantic slave trade as well as the slave trade in the Indian Ocean on the one hand, and slavery on the other, perpetrated from the fifteenth century onwards in the Americas and the Caribbean, in the Indian Ocean and in Europe against the African, Amerindian, Malagasy and Indian populations constitute a crime against humanity.

Article 2: School curricula and research programmes in history and the humanities will give the slave trade and slavery the important place they deserve. Cooperation that will make it possible to link the written archives available in Europe with the oral sources and archaeological knowledge accumulated in Africa, the Americas, the

---

37 A *"dwelling"* is a farm and manufacturing operation that grows, harvests, and processes mainly sugar and coffee. Sugar is, however, the dominant production of Guadeloupe. From 1848 onwards, factories were set up and, gradually, took over the entire manufacture of sugar.

38 An examination of the directory of deeds of the notary Auguste Thionville in Pointe-à-Pitre shows a large number of transactions of this type from 1850 onwards. (DPPC NOT GUA REP 38).

Caribbean and all other territories that have known slavery will be encouraged and promoted.

Article 3: A petition for recognition of the transatlantic slave trade as well as the Indian Ocean slave trade and slavery as a crime against humanity shall be submitted to the Council of Europe, international organisations and the United Nations. This request will also seek to find a common date at the international level to commemorate the abolition of the slave trade and slavery, without prejudice to the commemorative dates specific to each of the overseas departments.

7. Migrating to escape poverty

During the period 1800-1850, the Cestia were present in the islands of Guadeloupe and Puerto Rico, in the United States in Louisiana, and in metropolitan France, mainly in Nay, in the Pyrénées-Atlantiques, in the Gers and in the Hautes-Pyrénées.

More than 200 people [39] bore this surname between 1800 and 1850, almost the same number as for the following period, 1850 to 1900

The various migrations between 1800 and 1850

During the period 1800-1850 there were various migrations, internal migrations that could be professional, but also migrations to distant destinations, migrations of social conquest or economic success.

These movements take place in a context of significant transformation of society. In France and Europe, the *"industrial revolution"* of the nineteenth century shifted a predominantly agrarian and artisanal society to a commercial and industrial society. This revolution has its origins in discoveries and innovations that allow unprecedented

---

Excerpts from Jean Baptiste Noe's articles published by the newspaper L'Opinion in July 2017

"Louis-Philippe was enthusiastic about the Revolution, at least that of 1789-1792, not that of 1793. He adhered to this thirst for freedom, to this modernization of the kingdom, to this evolution towards a parliamentary monarchy. He is not far off, moreover, from having the same ideas as Louis XVI. The king wanted, with Turgot, to make the nobles pay and abolish privileges. They opposed it by blocking parliaments. Finally, the tax reform was carried out by force in the summer of 1789. It was nobles who, on August 4, mounted the tribune of the Assembly to demand the abolition of privileges. La Rochefoucauld, Noailles and the Duc d'Aiguillon, the three largest fortunes in the kingdom, much wealthier than the king, were elated on that August evening and voted for the abolition of privileges. »

"In this free trade defended by liberal thinkers, the idea of trust in men emerges. It is an anthropology based on spontaneous order, that is to say on the fact that by letting people do it, they end up setting up a just and harmonious society, turned towards the common good. Conversely, socialist thinkers are adepts of constructivism. They think of the ideal society, as it should be according to their views, and they do everything to apply it to others, despite their refusals or their adherences. This trust in man, this belief in the spontaneous order of society, leads to the creation of a society of trust, peace and freedom. Thus, unlike many of their contemporaries, liberals committed themselves to building pacifist movements and for the abolition of slavery. »

---

39 It is a census that could be called a "rolling census" because it is equal for a period to the number of people born before the end of the period and died after the beginning of the period. This is different from the enumeration at successive dates given on page 13

economic growth, stimulated by the progress of rail transport that changes trade relations and lifestyles. The liberal policy of the July Monarchy (1830-1848) accompanied this development favourably.

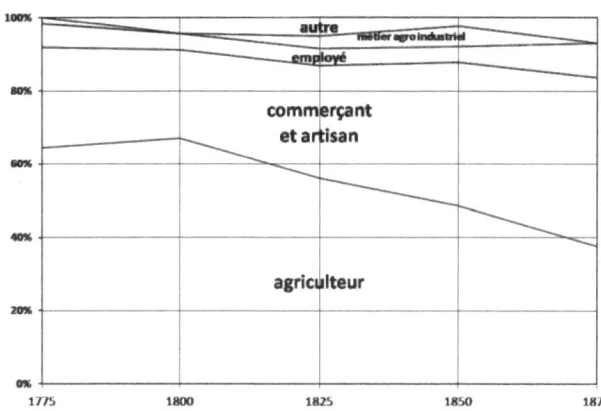

The observations made in the following paragraphs are not unrelated to this transformation of society. The Cestia moved, settled in a nearby village, abandoned their agricultural profession or embarked for America or the Caribbean. In this way, they participate in economic progress.

These migrations resulted in a change of profession [40]. The change of profession is in fact an indicator of the transformation of society. The graph opposite shows the evolution from 1775 to 1875 of the trades carried out by the bearers of the surname Cestia and its variants.

In this graph, the term farmer includes the professions of farmer, owner, brewer, day labourer, ploughman, sharecropper, winegrower. The category of merchant and craftsman refers to a wide variety of trades such as butcher, baker, café owner, butcher, carpenter, shoemaker, etc. The agro-industrial profession category concerns the occupations of the islands' settlers related to the production of sugar by slaves, such as inhabitants, house managers or merchants.

In 50 years, 20% of the population abandoned the agricultural trades and in 1850 it was about 5% of the same population of Cestia (100 people) who turned to the practice of slavery. This statistic concerns only those bearing the surname Cestia and its variants, but it can nevertheless be considered that this measure gives an indication of the evolution of the professional structure of Bigourdan society. Indeed, it seems difficult to admit that a patronymic name can induce a specific behavior.

The migrations observed are professional migrations, going to the city to get out of one's condition as a peasant, but also migrations that can be described as entrepreneurial, migrations of social conquest or economic success, accepting to go

---

40 The profession is transcribed in the various documents that have come down to us, civil status, notarial acts, census, etc.

far away to make a quick fortune, and also most often migrations that are both entrepreneurial and professional.

Internal migrations within the department concern towns and villages from Bigorre to the south of Gers.

Migrations to more distant horizons concern Argentina, particularly Buenos Aires, Louisiana and in particular the New Orleans region, Uruguay and more particularly Montevideo, the islands of Guadeloupe and Puerto Rico. Migrations to the Caribbean islands are much less known than those to South America.

It can be observed that if the departures to America are part of the history assumed and claimed of Bigorre, still celebrated today by cultural exchanges between Bigorre and America, the departures to the islands are not the subject, through memorial or cultural manifestations, of any testimony of the slavery history of Bigorre, although it is certainly very real.

I also note that for more than two centuries, the philosophers of the Enlightenment who inspired the values of our French Revolution, continue to transform the thinking and laws of our society: women's suffrage, laws on parity, debate on the tax advantages of deputies, etc. Collectively accepted morality therefore evolves slowly.

Thus Victor Schoelcher (Freemason journalist at the Grand Orient de France, writer and politician) who, in 1840, was an ardent defender of abolition, and who, in 1848, had the law of abolition passed, did he not say in 1830 "the negroes, issued from the hands of their masters with the ignorance and all the vices of slavery, would be good for nothing, neither for society nor for themselves" [41].

How can we doubt that what is today the consensus of the moral values of our society on which the law is based, is only the result of a slow evolution, when we also observe that Voltaire and Rousseau were not in favor of the education of the humble. Voltaire – , Philosopher of the Enlightenment! – said: *"Do not instruct the child of the villager, for it is not fitting for him to be taught."*. [42]

It therefore seems clear to me that the Cestia who lived in Guadeloupe in the nineteenth century and who practiced slavery are not, of course, those responsible for the slave system. They lived in a society that did not have the same consensus of values in the nineteenth century as those that drive us today.

We can therefore only note the paradox between the 2001 law, which characterizes, without any possibility of appeal, the actions of the colonists as "crimes against

---

41 "Revue de Paris", Journal critique politique et littéraire, 1830, page 82.

42 Emanuel Le Roy Ladurie, "The French Peasants of the Ancien Régime", 2015, Edition du Seuil. page 202.

humanity", and the laws applicable until 1848 which authorized the said colonists to practice slavery.

Robert Badinter in the program "Secrets d'Histoire Louis XIV, l'homme et le Roi" broadcast on November 14, 2017 at 9:00 p.m. with Stéphane Bern, declares about slavery at the time of Louis XIV: "The Code Noir legalizes the infamy of a system. We must not look at this with the legal codes of our time. We must take the measure of the century of Louis XIV to judge Louis XIV. »

Thus, it seems fair to me to leave to historians, and to them alone, the responsibility of granting or not, to the colonists who practiced slavery in compliance with the laws of the time, the mitigating circumstances of the judgment of History. This judgment can, in my opinion, only be detailed according to the places, the roles played and the times.

It is certain that the entire white population of the island at that time was, in fact, involved in slavery, a painful scourge of our history in France, a pain that is still felt today by those who are descendants of slaves.

This period in our history of France has long been a taboo subject, including in the families concerned. The 2001 law very judiciously encourages historians to study the delicate subject of slavery, even if it must be admitted that it is not up to the law to say what historians have to do. It is also necessary to be perfectly aware that while there are many historical sources concerning whites, they are much less so concerning slave populations.

If I have decided not to hide the following stories, which also concern my own ancestors, it is because I think that the descendants of colonists are in no way responsible for the actions of their ancestors, and that for this reason, even in the context of this very questionable past, the resentment of black descendants of slaves towards the descendants of colonists has no reason to exist. It seems to me, therefore, that without passion and anger, the facts must be examined and told.

8. From 1800 to 1850, getting out of poverty

Three brothers and a sister in Guadeloupe

When in 1800 Jean Cestia, aged 28, married Catherine Marie Burgues to Louit, he was not, as his descendants would be, a man who had already succeeded in business, or who had travelled the world. He was just the fifth of 5 children, a farmer like his father and grandfather.

Jean Cestia and Catherine Marie Burgues had 11 children. The first two of these siblings of 11 children, of whom only 8 reached adulthood, were Philippe dit Baylou n°4 and Pierre le n°6, then almost 10 years later in 1843, Philippe dit Bernard n°7 and his sister also named Philippe n°11 and the last born of the siblings.

At the beginning of the nineteenth century, technological and economic growth took hold and, from 1830 onwards, continued with the effects of the liberal policies of the July Monarchy. This economic boom, and more locally word of mouth, which worked well, made Louit's walls appear far too narrow to accommodate the ambitions of Jean and Catherine Cestia's children. The call of the islands is strong. We know that some succeed in this. Jean Cestia's children also know that Pierre and Martial, the brothers of their aunt Jeanne Fabares, have settled in Guadeloupe where they run the Dadons house of Victorine Aline Dadons, the wife of Martial Fabares. So many good family reasons to decide to leave, while the society of the time did not, like today's society, become aware of its crime of slavery practiced on the islands.

Bertrand Cestia

Bertrand Cestia (1805-1876), the second of 9 children, was born in Vic-en-Bigorre, a small town located about 20 km north of Tarbes. His father and grandfather are from Beccas in the Gers, a little more than 10 km from Vic. Following their marriage, his parents moved to Vic. Bertrand's aunt, Marie Cestia, was the wife of Jean Despalanques, a merchant in Pointe-à-Pitre who founded, around 1820, the company *"Despalanques et Cie"*, trading company between Bordeaux and Pointe-à-Pitre [43]. A trade

---

43 Until 1860, the "habitants" grew sugar cane and made sugar, which they sold on the spot to "merchants" who transported and resold the sugar in Bordeaux. Merchants imported tools, wines, cognacs, vinegars, cheese, clothing for slaves, corn, flour and especially cod to the island.

closely linked to the sugar agri-food industry: export of sugar and import of the products necessary for this industry.

At a very young age, Bertrand Cestia preferred his uncle's international trade to his father's butchery. He migrated in 1825 to Guadeloupe. Thus, according to the sources consulted, it is [44], the first bearer of the name Cestia to settle on the island where he met his first cousin Bertrand Carrere, hatter in Pointe-à-Pitre. But he also found other compatriots who had migrated before him to Guadeloupe, as well as those who, during the revolt of the Blacks, had fled Saint-Domingue to take refuge in Guadeloupe [45].

In Guadeloupe, Bertrand Cestia worked with his uncle Despalanques and quickly became his partner, then the company was expanded with the entry of Joseph Bordere brother-in-law of Bertrand Cestia known as *"the eldest"*, for he has a brother also named Bertrand dit *"the youngest"*. Bertrand Cestia, then created his own trading company with Nantes (Homberg and Homberg brothers) or Marseille.

In Guadeloupe, at that time, there was also Jean Brescon, a compatriot from Labatut-Rivière located 20 km north of Vic-en-Bigorre, who, at the end of his life, owned the castle of St Aunis in Vic-en-Bigorre, a castle he had bought for his retirement in France. Jean Brescon owned a large sugar house on the island *"The Crack"* of 140 keys. [46]. He died in April 1826, unmarried without children. His heirs are his 3 brothers, his 3 sisters and his 4 nephews. The deceased having made a will that favours two of his brothers, Pujo, one of Bertrand Cestia's brothers-in-law, mandated by the heirs not included in the will, has taken legal action to contest it.

But on January 4 and 5, 1827, an amicable agreement was reached on the spot between the heirs during a 2-day meeting held *"by triple daily shifts to accelerate, without any other interruptions than those of rest and sleep."*. The inventory of the Lézarde dwelling was also updated, an inventory where it was specified that *"a cow*

---

44 The notarial deeds of Guadeloupe available at the National Overseas Archives (ANOM) in Aix en Provence gave me a large amount of information concerning the commercial transactions of the Cestia in Guadeloupe in the nineteenth century. I have been able to note for the earlier periods the absence of Cestia in these archives.

45 In the eighteenth century, for economic reasons, the Bigourdans were mainly attracted to Saint-Domingue, then at the beginning of the nineteenth century to Guadeloupe. Following the violent revolts of the blacks in Santo Domingo, a number of Bigourdans (bourgeoisie and nobility) moved from Saint-Domingue to Guadeloupe at the end of the eighteenth century. Cf. Revue d'histoire de l'Amérique française Roger Massio, Professor at the College of Vic-en-Bigorre (Hautes-Pyrénées).

46 The number of slaves characterizes the importance of a dwelling. On average in 1830 a dwelling had 79 slaves. According to C Schnakenbourg, "The Crisis of the Slave System 1835-1847", page 22

and a heifer consumed for the meal at the present operation" were in deficit in the inventory.47]

The will of the deceased granted 2 shares each to his brother Jean-Baptiste de Paris and to his other brother Bertrand dit Bernard. In the end, the heirs agreed to receive each 1/7 of the castle of St Aunis and the proceeds of the sale of the house, and gave up the benefit of their parents' estate of Labatut-Rivière to the brothers Jean-Baptiste and Bertrand referred to in the will. It was agreed that the sugar estate would be administered until its sale by Bertrand Cestia and François Servient.

The inventory of 9 May 1826 is updated. We can therefore see that 12 slaves estimated at 10,507 Francs in fugitives [48] during the previous inventory have returned, and that 13 slaves have since gone on fugitives.

To reach this agreement, 5 of the 10 heirs made the trip to Guadeloupe: Jean-Baptiste came from Paris, Jeanne and Jeanne-Marie came from their native country accompanied by their two nieces who represent Marie Laffargue in the estate Deceased.

On January 4 and 5, no less than 14 people gathered at La Lézarde to seal these agreements for two whole days:

- as experts, two merchants, Pierre Desbordes and Bertrand Cestia. The latter is mandated by two heirs, Pierre and Bertrand, known as Bernard
- Jeanne Brescon married Darré, heiress from Libaros (near Tarbes)
- Jeanne Marie Brescon married Lamarque niece of the deceased from Labatut-Rivière, located about 10 km north of Vic-en-Bigorre.
- Jeanne Lafargue married Bonnet niece of the deceased, who came from Aurièbat, a commune which adjoins that of Labatut-Rivière
- Jean-Baptiste Brescon Jr. mandated by Jean Brescon the brother of the deceased
- Pascal Pujo embarked at Bordeaux for Guadeloupe on 26 October 1826. He was mandated by Marie Brescon wife Dubeau, sister of the deceased, and by Bernard and Anne Laffargue nephew and niece of the deceased,
- Etienne Richaud curator of vacant estates,
- Mr. Servient agent of the executor of the will,

---

47 See on genea-cestia.fr the transcription of the complete deed referenced: 1827-3 Brescon Estate - inventory inventory and various agreements.

48 Marronage: the state of a maroon slave, i.e. one who has regained his freedom by running away.

- Raveil de Fougères, R. Ageville and Félix Lecurieux Experts
- The Moirtin notaries and Cotin.

The affair of the brig Lightyear

Guadeloupe is far from the native country, it takes 6 to 8 weeks to reach Bordeaux. Thus, from his arrival in 1825 - he was 20 years old - to 1836, his return, Bertrand Cestia remained in Guadeloupe, probably without ever returning home. But contact by letter is frequent, especially for business, [49] but sometimes also for gossip or simply to give news.

Thus, in 1828, a letter from Bertrand Cestia to Despalanques evokes a slave trade affair [50]. In this letter, Bertrand Cestia evokes what he knew about the expedition; "The brig L'Éclair with a crew of 25 men must bring back 350 slaves, previously 312 slaves had been dealt with in fifteen days, 110 others even in five days!"

A local historian, Roger Massio, has, somewhat hastily on the basis of this correspondence, put Bertrand Cestia in charge of this expedition. This is absolutely not the case in view of the judicial

---

Letter from Pujo to Bertrand CESTIA

Bordeaux 5 August 1834

My dear brother-in-law,

At last the pegasus is about to leave, she is raising her jib this evening, I confirm my letter of July 10 by this ship and that of the 1st current by Europe; I am still without having received the dispatch of the deed of the enjoyment of Mr. Massignac, this delay comes from the receiver of the registration as soon as I am in my possession I will take advantage of the first opportunity to send it to you.

Prices are still very quiet 63.50 f The good, the coffees of Guadeloupe from 1.30 to 1.55 depending on their quality. The coasts of the harbour are no more advantageous.

For a long time Mr. Cestia Baylou [Philippe Cestia dit Baylou] has owed us 102.02 francs and Carrere for 4 to 5 years 143.25 francs. Please ask these gentlemen to give us these two sums; I have written to Mr. Cestia Baylou to this effect; As for our cousin, we have written to him several times as a result, our letters have always been unanswered.

Our father has completely retired to St Aunis, it has been decided I think to sell his boilers to Borderes, our sugars are still unsold because of their poor quality, I will still wait in the hope of an increase for later; we are going to drink a very bitter broth, it presents at this moment more than 3000 of losses

---

49 Most of Bertrand Cestia's epistolary archives disappeared in a fire. But Roger Massio, a local historian, was able to consult some of them before the fire.

50 Until 1831, the slave trade, although prohibited, was practiced with the complicit passivity of the authorities. But sometimes it went wrong...

archives [51] who tell us that this case ended up in court after the capture of the ship "L'éclair". A defect in the procedure saved the organizer of the expedition, a certain Morand, shipowner of the expedition and merchant of Port-Louis, to be condemned.

Business with the Cestia

In February 1831, Bertrand Cestia was in business with Pierre Cestia concerning a dwelling known as « *Champ d'Asile* » acquired by the latter in March 1830, a dwelling located in the commune of Sainte-Rose.

"Field of Asylum" What is it? Here is what Pierre Larousse writes: On the second return of Louis XVIII (after Waterloo, June 18, 1815), many Frenchmen, pursued by an implacable reaction, took refuge in the United States, where they were granted 100,000 acres of land on the Gulf of Mexico, between the Del Norte and Trinidad rivers, to found a colony. This place of refuge, this establishment for proscribed people, received the name of *"Field of Asylum."* The Sainte Rose habitation could have a link with that of the United States. [52]

The sale in Guadeloupe of this house also called Champ d'Asile de Bachelier to Pierre Cestia does not mention any slaves. However, to operate this 168-square-square coffee production house (about 160 ha), slaves were needed at that time; no other workforce is available, as Christian Schnackenbourg (Doctor of Law and Economics) explains *"Slavery became the only mode of production in the West Indies between 1660 and 1680, during the "sugar revolution" and it remained so until 1848. In a manufacturing economy with very little mechanization, such as that of Guadeloupe before the middle of the nineteenth century, it is in fact primarily on the number of men at work that the volume of production essentially depends.* » [53]

Since the end of the slave trade, there has been a shortage of slaves in Guadeloupe, especially in the sugar houses, and their price is rising. This led the owners of coffee or cocoa houses to sell their slaves to the highest bidders. The « *Champ d'Asile* » therefore had to be stripped of its slaves before being sold [54] to the young Pierre Cestia (17 years old) freshly arrived in Guadeloupe, but who probably already has an

---

51 Ledru Rollin, *"Journal du Palais Jurisprudence française",* volume XXIII 1830-1831, pages 1311 to 1314 and Patuis Dalloz editions, "Jurisprudence générale du Royaume", 1832, page 144.

52 According to an article in "*Genealogies and Caribbean History* ", this name "*Champ d'Asile*" may have a connection with the "*Champ d'Asile" domain* in Texas. (See Bulletin 10/86 Genealogy History of the Caribbean).

53 Christian Schnakenbourg, "The Crisis of the Slave System 1835-1847", 1980, L'Harmattan, page 46.

54 The Champ d'Asile house (160 ha) was sold for the price of 50,270 francs, of which 5,406 francs were payable in cash.

idea in mind concocted with Bertrand Cestia. (See "The affair of the brig Lightyear» page 69).

Indeed, in February 1831 Pierre and Bertrand Cestia and Jean-Baptiste Jammes (doctor of medicine) met at the notary Bornet's in Pointe-à-Pitre for the sale to Bertrand Cestia and J.B. Jammes by Pierre Cestia of three quarters of the house bought a little earlier, and for the creation of a company owned up to a quarter by Pierre Cestia and the rest in equal shares between the other two partners, company whose representatives are Bertrand Cestia and J.B. Jammes. The deed does not specify the purpose of the company, but it is easy to imagine that it was a structure to put this dwelling with slaves back into operation

Jean-Baptiste Jammes, originally from Orthez, would later become the mayor of Goyave, a commune in Guadeloupe, and above all the grandfather of the famous poet Francis Jammes. Jean-Baptiste Jammes was buried in 1857 on the Champ d'Asile dwelling in Sainte-Rose.

But this association, concluded in February 1831, did not last. In July of the same year, the same people met before a notary in Pointe-à-Pitre to terminate the previous contract in return for an indemnity of 5,406 francs paid to Pierre Cestia. The young Pierre Cestia then found himself the sole owner of a 190-hectare estate with payment deadlines over several years. In April 1832, he in turn terminated the sale by which he had become the owner.

Returning home

In 1832, Bertrand Cestia, 30 years old, began to prepare for his retirement and his return to his country. He freed his slave Zabeth, 63 years old, and undertook, as required by law, to provide for his needs.

Then, in 1833, from the heirs of Jean Brescon, who died in Guadeloupe in 1826, he bought the estate of Saint-Aunis in Vic-en-Bigorre (now known as the castle of Saint Aunis).

He did not immediately occupy this beautiful and large residence surrounded by a vast agricultural estate of generous land. However, his brother-in-law stayed there in 1834, before embarking for America. He then wrote to Bertrand Cestia: *"I stayed with you, in Saint-Aunis, where I admired this beautiful property with great pleasure. You have the finest maize in all of Bigorre, you will have from 150 to 200 hectolitres [55]; there will even be enough wine despite the frost".*

In 1836, Bertrand Cestia, after 10 years spent on the islands, returned to Vic-en-Bigorre. In 1854, at the age of 48, he became mayor of the commune of Pujo, located

---

55 Maize cultivation developed in the Hautes-Pyrénées from 1830, while this crop, introduced in the eighteenth century, had remained stationary until then.

5 km south of Vic in the immediate vicinity of his residence in St Aunis, whose estate straddled the two communes. In March 1859, Bertrand Cestia, the son of the butcher of Vic, became a notable; he was admitted to the Academic Society of the Hautes-Pyrénées proposed as a resident member by two members of the said society. He remained the mayor of his commune for 20 years.

Pierre Cestia

Pierre at the age of 17, and Philippe his brother at the age of 24, probably left together around 1830. As soon as he arrived, he embarked on a partnership project with Bertrand Cestia de Vic and Jean-Baptiste Jammes, which ultimately failed (see "Business with the Cestia» page 70) but which will allow Pierre Cestia to be compensated with 5,400 francs. A nice sum that represents more than 10% of the purchase price of a 160-hectare estate. The breach of this agreement, which, given the amount of the indemnity, is most certainly the result of a serious breach, is possibly linked to the absence of the slaves necessary for the exploitation of this estate.

In March 1847, the three brothers Philippe Baylou, a house manager and owner, living in the commune of Port Louis, Philippe dit Bernard, a house manager also living in the commune of Port Louis, and Pierre, also a manager living in the same commune, were at their notary Alexis Lemoine Maudet's in Port Louis. They entrusted Mrs. Veuve Guillemat to a representative born Demoiselle Ducos, owner, living in Tarbes, the management of 3/8 of their parents' property which comes to them as an inheritance.

Philippe Cestia aka Baylou

Philippe Baylou, who arrived on the island of Guadeloupe in 1830, was first a merchant until his marriage to Marie Anne Zeline Dumornay in June 1836. Marie Anne Zeline Dumornay Matignon was born in Guadeloupe; she is the daughter of a settler and a widow without children.

In 1836, "Baylou", as he was then called, was already a small, well-established landowner, which allowed him to buy back indirectly from his wife the inheritance of 10,000 Francs that she had inherited from her aunt Sophie and which she had to part with to pay off debts. Pierre Fabares de Louit helped Philippe to clean up the financial situation. Pierre Fabares is the brother of Jeanne Fabares wife of Martial Cestia uncle of Philippe de Louit. He has been living in Guadeloupe for several years now. Pierre Fabares bought the inheritance from Zéline, valued at 9,800 francs, consisting of various movable assets, including two adult slaves, valued at 2,000 francs, and a one-storey wooden house on a 900 m² plot of land, valued at 6,000 francs. Then two weeks later, Pierre Fabares sold everything at the same price to Philippe. This double transaction allowed his wife to repay her debts and allowed him to become the owner of his wife's property.

With the small home of his wife, who was 12 years older than him and a widow without children, Philippe returned to his job as a farmer. The house located in the commune of Port-Louis had only 25 hectares of land and only 3 young slaves aged 14, 4 and 2. The presence in the inventory of the marriage contract of two slaves aged 2 and 4 seems to be in violation of the law which forbade the separation of slave children from their mothers before the age of 14.

Here again, the small number of slaves in relation to the surface area of land shows that his wife's home had suffered greatly from the sugar crisis that was raging at the time, a crisis due to overproduction, the increase in the price of slaves and the progression of the idea of abolition among the servile populations, which led to a decrease in the productivity of slaves.

In 1843, an earthquake almost completely destroyed Pointe-à-Pitre, located 30 km south of Port-Louis. An ordeal that adds to the difficulties already present.

In 1845, Philippe accepted the management of the property of Victor Jean Pierre Félix Victor Saux doctor living in the town of Port-Louis, which contributed to his social and economic progress.

Thus, Philippe's business progressed. He borrowed money from Despalanques de Vic, former partner and uncle of Bertrand Cestia, and was thus able to invest in slaves. He was also the manager of a large sugar refinery, known as St Pierre, of 280 ha owned by Jean-Baptiste Philibert St Pierre from Lamothe-Landerron in Gironde.

At the time of the abolition of slavery, Philip owned 23 slaves who allowed him to properly operate his wife's home. For the loss of his slaves he was compensated by the state by an annuity over 20 years (see «Colonial indemnity in Guadeloupe» *page 59*59) whose transfer enabled him to repay Despalanques' debt of 4,400 francs and to receive the balance, i.e. 5,000 francs. [56].

In the middle of the nineteenth century, Guadeloupe's years of prosperity came to an end. Many decide to return to the country. But the Cestia de Louit seem attached to this island and stay.

Thus, Jean-Baptiste Philibert de St Pierre, for whom Philippe was the manager of his home, returned to Lamothe Landerron in Gironde. He is therefore looking for a successor to manage his home. It is Philippe Cestia who is chosen. In January 1850,

---

56 On 13 December 1850 in Pointe-à-Pitre in Guadeloupe, Philippe Cestia of Port-Louis pledged to Jean Despalanque of Vic en Bigorre, represented by Bernard Bustigeat of Pointe-à-Pitre, the entire amount of his annuity, i.e. about 9,000 francs, obtained for the emancipation of 23 slaves on 27 May 1848. Taking into account a debt of 4,400 francs contracted with Despalanque, he immediately received the sum of 5,000 francs in exchange. Philippe Cestia retained his rights in the Banque de Prêt et d'Escompte à la Guadeloupe, created by deduction of one-eighth of the annuities allocated.

Philippe concluded a farm lease for a gross third of the fruit for 5 full and consecutive years from 15 July 1849. The annual production of raw sugar is estimated at 30 tons, 10 of which go to the lessor.

In 1854, when Pierre Fabares succeeded originally from Louit, Philippe Cestia was appointed as subrogated tutor of Arthur Martial Pierre Charles Fabares, his *"nephew"* [57] son of Martial Fabares. The young Fabares is the heir of Pierre Fabares by representation of his father Martial, brother of the deceased.

In 1855, Philippe died in Port-Louis without descendants, aged 46. He leaves a widowed wife for the second time.

Philippe Cestia, known as Bernard

Philippe Cestia, known as Bernard (see diagram of filiation below) obtained a visa for Guadeloupe on 14 March 1843, one month after the earthquake in Pointe-à-Pitre on 8 February 1843. No doubt a coincidence that will allow him to help his brother repair the damage as soon as he arrives on the island.

Philippe, known as Bernard, did not stay very long on the island and after the death of his brother, he decided to return to the country, but not without having first received the colonial indemnity for the few slaves in whom he had invested to work on his brother's dwelling until the abolition of slavery in 1848.

Shortly after his return, he married, in November 1856 in Louit, Magdelaine Dortignac who is 19 years old. He is 41 years old...

In 1857 and 1864, his sons Honoré Jean Marie (my AGP) and Auguste Sylvain were born.

Philippe Cestia, like many of those who returned from the islands, became a notable of his commune. Officially, he declared himself an annuitant in the 1856 and 1861 censuses. But in 1866 he declared himself a farmer like his father and grandfather... The islands were already far away! Elected mayor of Louit in 1865, re-elected in 1870, he remained mayor until his death in 1874.

The Cestia de Louit in the islands of Guadeloupe and Puerto Rico

To succeed in business in the islands, you need to rely on support from acquaintances or family. The Cestia can count on the family clan to help them prosper.

Philippe Cestia married Carrere
If the name Philippe is now an exclusively masculine name, it was also sometimes given to girls in the nineteenth century.

---

57 In fact, Arthur Martial, Pierre Charles Fabares was the nephew of Jeanne Fabares, wife of Martial Cestia, paternal uncle of Philippe Cestia.

Mademoiselle Philippe, the last of 8 siblings at the time of her birth, sister of Philippe dit Baylou, Philippe dit Bernard and Pierre, left the family home in Louit before she was 14 years old where the effects of her 3 brothers' visit to the islands had not yet really been felt. Traditional Bigorre, i.e. excluding the effect of immigration, is a poor region. Jean and Catherine Burgues are certainly not very rich. Miss Philippe was therefore probably placed as a servant at an age when many girls went to work in the city. And so at a very young age, before her 18th birthday, she married Jean Pierre Carrere, a blacksmith.

Our Miss Philippe had never lived in Guadeloupe, but we met her, in April 1840, when she was 18 years old, at a notary's office in Port-Louis for a financial transaction with her first cousin Pierre Cestia of Louit, son of Martial Cestia. Pierre was living in Puerto Rico and happened to be passing through Port-Louis in Guadeloupe at the time.

After the death in 1847 of Jean Cestia, the father of our Philippe Cestia, Louit's house is quite empty. The family farm is run by Emmanuel and his sister Catherine, son and daughter of Jean Cestia, who have always remained in Louit. And when Emmanuel died in July 1851, Philippe, her husband Jean Pierre Carrere and his parents-in-law settled for a while in Louit with Philippe, his brother, who had returned from Guadeloupe. After the marriage of his brother Philippe in November 1856, his sister left Louit's house to her brother and his young wife Magdelaine Dortignac.

Catherine and Pierre Cestia
Catherine and Pierre Cestia are the daughter and son of Martial Cestia de Louit, husband of Fabares,

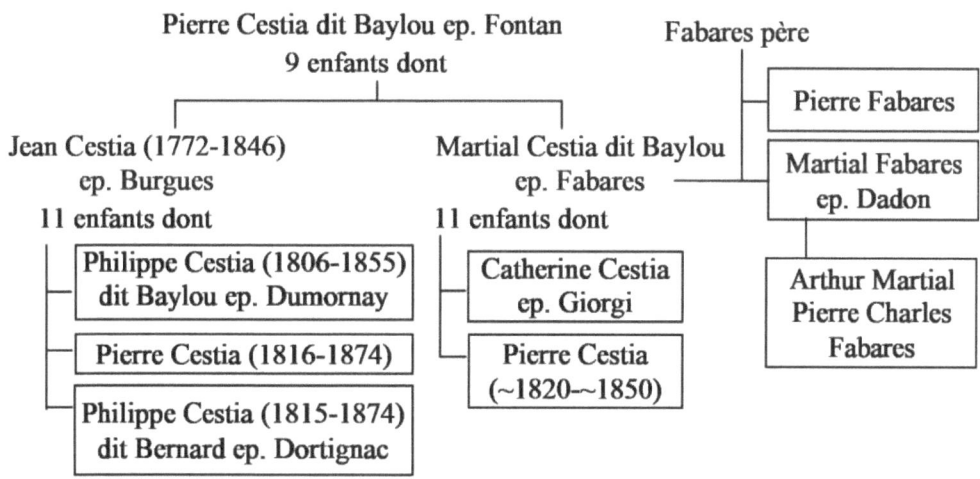

From 1800 to 1850, getting out of poverty

Pierre was the last of 11 children, 10 of whom reached adulthood. His father and grandfather, named Pierre like him, were both mayors of their commune of Louit. Catherine n°6, born in July 1805, was about 10 years older than Pierre.

His father Martial was a robust person since he reached the age of 80, which at the time was rare. Martial was able to give his children a solid education that allowed his son Pierre to become a doctor.

Pierre and Catherine were attracted to the islands like their first cousins from Louit, Philippe Bailou, Philippe dit Bernard and Mlle Philippe, thus following the example of their uncle Fabares

Before the ages of 25 and 35 respectively, they probably migrated together to the island of Puerto Rico where they settled in Mayaguez, located at the western end of the island.

From there, shortly after his arrival in Mayaguez, Pierre went to Guadeloupe where he met his cousin Germaine Philippe, who was passing through Port-Louis, for a financial transaction involving the *"transfer",* which today would be called a transfer to his benefit, of a sum of money of 13,000 gourdes, or about 16,000 francs at the time. This was a significant sum of money since a few years earlier his cousin Pierre had been able to acquire a 190-hectare estate for 50,000 francs. Unfortunately, we have not found out what type of agreement between the parties this money transfer corresponds to.

August 31, 1843 Pierre Cestia accompanied his sister Catherine to the altar of the Church of Our Lady of the Candlestick in the city of Mayaguez, Puerto Rico for her wedding to Angel Toussaint Giorgi. He is 27 years old. She is 38. He was born in Corsica in Farinole, located in the north of the island, a few kilometers west of Bastia.

A few years after the death of both her parents, Catherine went to Louit, her native village, with her husband Ange Toussaint Giorgi, to settle her parents' estate. Pierre does not make the journey; he is represented by his brother-in-law Giorgi.

Later, Ange Toussaint retired to his native village in Corsica with Catherine, who lived there until the age of 70.

Louis Cestia
Louis Cestia was born in Lescurry in 1836. His father and grandfather were farmers there; they are the Cestia Coutillou de Lescurry. In 1853, at the age of 17, Louis embarked for Guadeloupe. I have not discovered any trace of his passage on the island in the notaries' archives, nor any family or neighborhood ties with settlers who left before him.

In the second half of the nineteenth century, after abolition, success was difficult in Guadeloupe, especially without belonging to a family or business clan.

Louis Cestia, who was then living in Saint-François, located at the eastern end of Grande-Terre, died at the age of 37 in Trois-Rivières, located at the southern end of Basse-Terre, in the house of Adolphe Silver, far from his home and his native village.

François Cestia

On 8 September 1860, François Cestia, aged 17, born in Lescurry and working as a farmer there, obtained a visa granted by the Prefect of Gironde and a passport, obtained from the Tarbes authorities on 1 September 1860. Destination Guadeloupe Island, on the ship "Bon Père" which left the port of Bordeaux on September 13, 1860. It was a three-masted ship of 248 tons, commanded by Captain Noge, assisted by a crew of 11 men. It flies the French flag, its home port is Bordeaux.

He left at the age of 18 before the military census of 20-year-olds. He was therefore declared insubordinate in 1864. But in Guadeloupe it benefits from the application of Article 16 of the law of 27 July 1872: "Young people whose infirmities make them unfit for any active or auxiliary service in the army are exempt from military service."

His infirmity does not prevent François Cestia, thanks to his talent, to quickly become a rentier. He met Marie Cécile Eugénie Aquart-Pieton of whom, Louise Clermonthe-Rouil, the mother-in-law (first companion of her father Eugène Hubert Pieton a sugar industrialist) was a slave, freed before the birth of her 3 children, all of whom were recognized by their father Eugène Hubert Pieton. Marie Cécile Eugénie was the daughter of Modestine Aquart second wife of his father. Louise Clermonthe-Rouil's mother, Scholastique, never had a surname. It was also freed in 1833.

Thus Marie Cécile Eugénie married François Cestia, had a half-sister and 2 half-brothers born between 1837 and 1847 to a mother who had been a slave until 1833.

Around 1880, 20 years after his departure, François Cestia returned to his native village where he settled with his partner after a few years in Bordeaux. In 1883, in Lescurry, their daughter Marie Eugénie Denise Cestia was born, who was recognized by her father within a month of her birth. His father died three years later.

The Cestia in Louisiana from 1800 to 1850

The economic decline of the island of Guadeloupe from 1835 onwards encouraged migration to Louisiana, where trade allowed rapid success and integration facilitated by a large community of French people in this sector of activity.

Bertrand Cestia, the son of the butcher of Vic, who retired to Pujo at the castle of Saint Aunis, was the second of 9 children, all born in Vic-en-Bigorre between 1803 and 1820, 6 of whom reached adulthood. The eldest, Marie, remained in Vic like her sister Rosalie. The other 4 left Vic and went to seek their fortune in Guadeloupe and Louisiana.

Bertrand Cestia (1810-1885) known as the younger, and in his family says Adolphe, married in New Orleans around the age of 30. Like his brother in Guadeloupe, he is

> New Orleans in the nineteenth century
>
> Rue Royale, rue de Chartres, rue Toulouse, the Ursuline convent, the French Quarter, the French Market, so many names of streets, buildings, and places that inscribe the French presence in New Orleans in the urban fabric. Founded by Bienville in 1718. Named in honor of the Regent of France, New Orleans was both a French foundation, the capital of Louisiana, and the major penetration route for French culture and French settlers into the region.
>
> The population of New Orleans, like many cities in the United States and Europe, experienced very strong growth in the nineteenth century. The city grew from about 20,000 inhabitants in 1810 to 168,000 in 1860 and 280,000 in 1900. In this context, the numerical importance of French immigrants in New Orleans, a city that was growing rapidly, quickly faded, to the point of representing only 6.4% of the inhabitants in 1850, 4.6% in 1870 and only 1.6% in 1900.
>
> More than 45% of French immigrantsare retail merchants and 20% are merchants, while only 20% and 10% of Louisianans respectively fall into these categories. Thus, a travel account published in 1828 showsthis French domination in the city's merchant sector: "French emigrants are numerous in New Orleans. Among them are many very respectable merchants, a few lawyers, doctors. In 1835, another traveller to New Orleansobserved: "As one approaches the market, the French shopsbecome dominant, to the point that one could imagine, aided by the sound of the French language, the French faces and the French goods on all sides, crossing a street in Le Havre or Marseilles." »
>
> Marjorie Bourdelais "French Immigrants in New Orleans in the Nineteenth Century: A Long Stability of Forms of Integration"

in commerce and trade. Bertrand arrived in New Orleans in 1837. He was the first Cestia to migrate to Louisiana. He is joined by Jean-Alphe Cestia who is not a close relative, but is a native of Vic like him. It is therefore likely that they formed a relationship. Bertrand Cestia returned to Vic, probably after his widowhood, around 1876.

Jeanne Marie Cestia (1812-1881) from Vic, the sister of the two Bertrands, one the elder and the other the younger, married Paul Pujo. They settled in Bordeaux where their daughter Anaïs was born in 1829. It was then that they left for New Orleans where they were probably joined by the brother and brother-in-law Bertrand. Paul Pujo was in the merchant business and he probably worked with his two brothers-in-law, the two Bertrands. But it seems that life in New Orleans did not please Jeanne Marie, who returned to Vic and married Dominique Daveran in 1838 with whom she had a son Jean Léopold.

Enfin Louise (1820-1882) the youngest of the siblings, embarked for New Orleans around 1850 where she lived for a while, but finally settled in New Iberia, where the children of Jean Alphe Cestia, his compatriot from Vic, were settled.

Another of Vic's compatriots, Paul Bernard Cestia, not related to the children of the butcher of Vic, migrated to New Orleans around 1850. Also unrelated, Laurent Sestiaa, originally from Nay, migrated to New Orleans in 1828 at the age of 30.

The Cestia in France from 1800 to 1850

Basses-Pyrénées (Pyrénées-Atlantiques)
The Cestia of this large family of Nay work in the textile industry for 50% of them, 20% of whom are more precisely in the wool industry, then come carpenters for 30% and finally craftsmen and shopkeepers for 20%. The observations made for the period 1800-1850 in Nay are very similar to those of the following period 1850-1900 The Cestia de Nay were craftsmen and workers who knew the hard life of the proletariat in the nineteenth century, and who were the actors of the industrial revolution and the economic boom of the nineteenth century. This is a far cry from the economic success of the Cestia in the islands of Guadeloupe or Puerto Rico or Louisiana.

In Nay in the period 1800-1850 there are four branches of Sestian,
- the branch of first cousins whose grandfather was Jean Sestian, married Anglade,
- then the branches from Jean Sestian married to Gouailles,
- of Guilhaume Sestian married Darric,
- and finally that of Pierre Jean married Pehourtic.

There are also five branches whose grandfathers are Sestiaa:
- the grandchildren of Jean Sestiaa, married Barthes,
- of Pierre Sestiaa, husband of Pardilhon,
- of Jean Sestiaa, husband of Mesplet,
- Bernard Sestiaa husband Latapie,
- and finally of Jean Sestiaa, husband of Barthes.

We also have the ten grandchildren of Jean Pierre Sestia, husband and wife Poey and those of Jean Sestia, husband of Abbadie. During this period, the fifteen grandchildren of Bernard Cestia, married to Lajusa, also lived in Nay (including Claracq). and the three grandchildren of Jean Cestiaa, married to Bergeret. We also have the ten grandchildren of Jean Pierre Sestia, husband and wife Poey and those of Jean Sestia, husband of Abbadie. During this period, the fifteen grandchildren of Bernard Cestia, married to Lajusa, also lived in Nay (including Claracq). and the three grandchildren of Jean Cestiaa, married Bergeret.

In Bayonne was born Sestiant (with a final t) Anne (1748-1808) daughter of Sestian Jean, gardener and winegrower from Lescurry. Anne's sister, meanwhile, was born in Arcangues, more than 100 km south of Bayonne. After his birth, his father came to settle in Lescurry, his native village, and had three children from his second marriage, only one of whom Bernard Cestian (1760-1854) known as Coubé will reach adulthood. The movement of families over such a great distance in France was rare at that time.

Gers

Jean Cestia dit Coutillou (1734-1818) was born in Beccas to a family originally from Lescurry. In 1764 he married Beccas Geneviève Jeanne Becas. A surname that could lead one to believe that it is a long-standing family of Beccas, but it is not the case. His father was from Buzon, located a few kilometres north of Beccas. Between 1765 and 1786, Jean Cestia and his wife had six children, including Arnaud and his sister Marie n° 3 and 4 of the siblings. Arnaud who became the mayor of Malabat, while Marie who married Despalanques lived for some time in Guadeloupe.

The n°1 and 2 of the siblings were born in Villecomtal-sur-Arros but the following were all born in Beccas. Jeanne-Marie, the eldest, married Jean Carrère of Buzon where she settled. The No. 2 of the siblings, Bertrand, known as the eldest, joined his brother Jean, the No. 5 of the siblings, a butcher in Vic-en-Bigorre, in Vic. No. 6 Jean moved to Vic where he worked as a janitor.

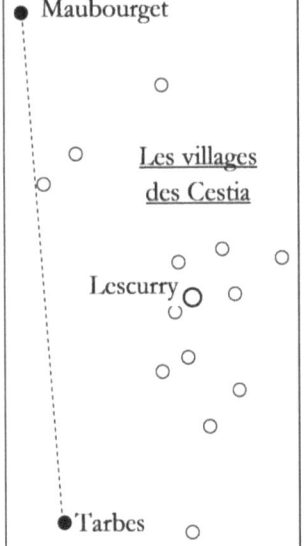

Hautes-Pyrénées

Lescurry, Vic-en-Bigorre, Louit and Dours were the villages and towns of the Cestia at the beginning of the nineteenth century. However, most often, the Cestia did not take root in these towns and villages, they migrated to other communes: Artagnan, Buzon, Castelvieilh, Castera-Lou, Sénac, Lacassagne, Lansac, Peyrun, Pouyastruc, Saint-Sever-de-Rustan. These villages are located north and south of Lescurry and east of a Tarbes Maubourget line.

Lescurry

In 1806, there were 290 inhabitants in this small town located on the side of a hill. Fifty years later, there are only 90 more. The topography of the commune, which is not very favourable to cultivation, explains this modest demographic growth compared to that observed in the neighbouring communes.

The Cestia de Lescurry are *"growers"* for 80% of them and for 20%. *"ploughmen"* and therefore owners.

Between 1800 and 1850 there were four families (18 to 20 people) who bore the surnames Cestia or Cestian. They are the families of Guillaume Cestian, husband of Marthe Dumestre, Jean Cestian dit Coutillou married Anne Defes, Bernard Raymond Cestia married Jeanne Durac and Denis Damien Cestia, husband of Michèle Baru. The children of these couples, married between 1755 and 1831 in Lescurry, had a total of 27 children, of whom only 21 reached adulthood.

This assessment of the infant mortality of the four families who lived in Lescurry between 1800 and 1850 illustrates the mortality and life expectancy at the beginning of the nineteenth century.

Vic-en-Bigorre

In 1806, the small town of Vic had 3,889 inhabitants, and in 1872 it had only 3,397 inhabitants.[58] This decrease is not observed for the surname Cestia, whose representation in Vic increased from 10 to 19 from 1800 to 1850.

Migration to the city led to a change of profession. In 1850, only 21% of them were farmers or ploughmen in Vic, while in the same period in Lescurry, a rural village, 80% of them practiced these trades. In Vic, in 1850, 14% were "annuitants", we would say today retired. The other trades were mason, carpenter, butcher, merchant, janitor, servant or seamstress, activities that only the small town could offer and that the Cestia who settled there came for.

But if Vic attracts the Cestias, it is also because it is from there that they leave for Libourne or Bergerac to practice new jobs or much further away in the wide world to try to make a quick fortune, in Louisiana, Argentina and Guadeloupe. It is perhaps this desire to travel the world that explains the decrease in the population of Vic at a time when cities generally experience growth due to what is usually called the "*rural exodus*". The attractiveness of the city of Tarbes, whose population increased from 7,934 inhabitants in 1806 to 25,146 in 1886, probably also explains the lesser interest in the small town of Vic-en-Bigorre. Thus Vic-en-Bigorre in the nineteenth century (from 1806 to 1872) seemed to have difficulty resisting competition from Tarbes, while the population of Vic decreased by 13%, that of Tarbes increased by 217%.

---

58 Sources: departmental archives of the Hautes-Pyrénées.

Louit

In the nineteenth century, Louit was a small rural commune of about 185 inhabitants whose population remained stable during the period 1806-1886. On the western part, stony hillsides were favourable to the cultivation of vines, *"wine culture"* according to the expression used by the teacher in his 1887 monograph, while in the eastern plain the clay soil favoured the cultivation of wheat and corn.

The law of 14 December 1789 organised democratic representation in the 44,000 municipalities of France.

"Active citizens" elect the members of the "municipal body" who elect their "leader", the mayor.

To be "active citizens" one must be French over 25 years old, reside in the canton, pay a direct contribution of at least three days of work, and not be a domestic servant or hired servant.

Thus, in 1789, citizens were equal, but some were still "more equal than others", as Coluche would say much later.

Direct taxes were established in 1791 by the Constituent Assembly. There are three of them: the land tax, which covers all land, the personal and movable tax, which covers all income not derived from trade or land, and the patent tax, which taxes professions according to external signs.

The municipal body appoints twice the number of members of the municipal body. These notables form, with the members of the municipal body, the general council of the commune, and will be called only for important matters.

Pierre Cestia, my grandfather, is a farmer, a ploughman who owns the land he cultivates. After the revolution, in 1793, he was elected a member of the municipal general council and mayor of his commune. On his birth certificate, he is Cestia, but he is Sesthian on his marriage certificate.

At the beginning of the year 1800, there was Louit, the family of Pierre Cestia dit Baillou (Bayou) and his wife Marie Fontan, a family composed of Pierre and Marie and their three children: Martial, who was 33 years old and had a daughter Jeanne Marie, aged 2, Jean, known as the youngest, 28 years old, who married in August 1800, and Pascal, who remained unmarried.

Pierre's son, Martial, was elected municipal councillor of Louit on 21 March 1816. In 1865 and 1870, it was Philippe, Pierre's grandson, Jean's son, who, following in his father's footsteps, was elected mayor of Louit.

Between 1800 and 1822, the two brothers Jean (1772-1846) and Martial (1767-1848) each had 11 children, of whom, for Jean, 8 reached adulthood, and 9 for Martial. So a total of 17 children who could have contributed to increasing the population of the village, if migration had not thwarted this perspective.

In 1850, of Martial's 6 living children, only Dominiquette and Jeanne-Marie remained in Louit. Because Catherine is in Puerto Rico, Bernarde got married in Saint-Sever-de-

Rustan, Jean is married to Artagnan and Jeanne Marie in Lescurry. On the same date, out of Jean's 6 living children, Louit only had Catherine, Emmanuel and her sister Philippe, who had already returned from Guadeloupe by that date. Their three brothers, Philippe, Philippe dit Bernard and Pierre, are still in Guadeloupe.

So, despite two large families of 11 children, the Cestia de Louit were no more numerous in 1850 than they were in 1800!

Dours

Formerly *"Dours-en-Bigorre"*, is a small village situated, at an altitude of about 290 metres, on a fertile hill which extends from north to south and dominates the plain of Tarbes to the west, and on the east side the valley of Loulès.

In his 1887 monograph, the teacher of Dours speaks of his commune with passion: "Straddling a beautiful hill, the first coming from the west, Dours enjoys a magnificent view. Its horizon extends on one side to the Pyrenees, whose blue hue is magnificent, on the other to the hills bordering the Basses-Pyrénées, covered with wood or heather and crowned by a few rare houses. On a beautiful summer day the site is most picturesque. The Pyrenees are first of all eye-catching. In front of the spectator, the valley of Campan emerges, the edges of which his imagination willingly crosses, and descends the buttresses which descend imperceptibly to give birth to the plain. Then his eye is lost on the vast and luxuriant plain of Bigorre, covered with beautiful harvests and where beautiful villages are spread out, half hidden in the trees."

In 1806 there were 157 inhabitants in Dours, thirty years later there were more than 300, believing that the inhabitants of Dours had the same passion for their village as their teacher.

In Dours as in Louit, stony hillsides are favourable to the cultivation of vines, while in the plain the clay soil favours the cultivation of wheat and maize. A topography favorable to culture that leads to a lower attraction for America, which may also explain the population growth.

Between 1800 and 1850, the Cestia de Dours family belonged to the family of Jacques, married to Saint-Ubery. Jacques Cestia, known as Saucette, a labourer, married Anne Saint-Ubery in 1806. In 1815 Jacques bought the Château de Dours, the former seigniorial residence. Between 1809 and 1826 they had 7 children, only 5 of whom reached adulthood: Jean became a shoemaker, Marie married in Dours, Michel was a ploughman in Dours like his father and Paul Hyppolite the youngest married in Castelvieilh and settled there.

To the next generation, Jean Cestia, known as Jacques for he is the son of Jacques, is a shoemaker. He married Jacquette Tardivailh in 1840. Between 1842 and 1854, they had 5 children. The two eldest children, Bernard a baker, and Jacques a shoemaker, migrated to Buenos Aires, Argentina. The two daughters Félicité and

Marie, as well as the youngest Adolphe Blaise remained in Dours. Finally the fourth, Michel Cestia farmer, farmer, married Marie Duffau in 1846. They have 3 children. Marie, the eldest, married in Dours, like her two brothers, Paul Felix and Jean Marie, a labourer, who were both farmers like their father.

Artagnan

We find Jean Cestia in Artagnan, the son of Martial Cestia de Louit. He has, in Artagnan with Domenga, 3 boys and two girls. The youngest, Gabriel, a baker, married in Villecomtal-sur-Arros where he had a son and a daughter. But before his marriage in the 1881 military census, he was 20 years old, he drew the N°1. He therefore had to devote 4 years of his life to the military cause. In 1882, he was incorporated into the 3rd Infantry Regiment of the Navy. In 1883 and 1884 he was in Cochinchina (now Vietnam). Then in Formosa (Taiwan), he participated in the Kelung military campaign in 1885 and 1886. He received the Military Medal of Tonkin in 1886.

Jean Sestia also settled in Artagnan and his wife Marie Gardey. Jean comes from much further away, he was born in Nay. He decided to leave the large industrial city of the Basses-Pyrénées (Pyrénées-Atlantiques) to set up as a tavern owner in the large village of d'Artagnan, which then had between 700 and 900 inhabitants.

Buzon

In Buzon we meet Marie-Anne Cestia, the daughter of Michel Cestia de Dours, who married in this small village of less than 400 inhabitants to Honoré Rives, an innkeeper. We also find Jeanne-Marie Cestia, the daughter of Jean Cestian dit Coutillou, a labourer from Beccas (see page 80), who married Jean Carrere in Buzon.

Castelvieilh

In Castelvieilh, we meet Paul Hyppolite Cestia who married in 1851 and had 8 children with Justine Bordis.

Castera-Lou

We meet Louis Cestia again farmer from Lescurry who married Jeanne Duffau in 1847 in Castera-Lou. They had 5 children, including Louis who became mayor of Castéra-Lou in 1869.

Sénac

Jean Cestian dit Coubé de Lescurry married in Sénac in 1785 where he had 4 children with Marguerite Cougot.

Lacassagne

Antoine Cestia de Sénac, son of Jean Cestia married in Lacassagne in 1845. Jean-Marie Cestia de Lescurry married in Lacassagne in 1843. He has a child with his wife Dominiquette Roques.

Lansac
In Lansac we meet Jean Sestia farmer, ploughman, son of Jean Sestian and Domenges Daubes In 1853 Jean Sestia married Marie Darre who gave him 6 children, 4 of whom reached adulthood: 3 girls and 1 boy who himself had two daughters in Lansac.

Peyrun
Marie Cestius de Lescurry, after her marriage in her native village, settled in Peyrun, a small village of less than 300 inhabitants, with her husband Bernard Mothe dit Trandolle.

Pouyastruc
In Pouyastruc, a small town of about 700 inhabitants, we meet Dominiquette Bernarde Cestia the daughter of Martial de Louit who married Adolphe Gardey there.

Saint-Sever-de-Rustan
In Saint-Sever-de-Rustan, a small town of about 600 inhabitants, we find another daughter of Martial Cestia de Louit who married François Nougues.

9. Conscription in France from 1789 to 1998

Before the French Revolution, the army was made up of volunteers, non-volunteer militias, foreign regiments and the nobility. The Revolution only kept a recruitment of volunteers. But this method of recruitment is proving insufficient. In 1793, a partial requisition was organized among citizens aged 25 to 40, single or widowed without children, by drawing lots or elections. The situation was critical, the decree of 23 August 1793 proclaimed *"From this moment, until the moment when the enemies have been driven from the territory of the Republic, all French people are in permanent requisition for the service of the army"*

This exceptional regime was replaced on 5 September 1798 by compulsory military service for unmarried and widowed 20 to 25 year olds without children, which complemented the recruitment of volunteers. This law, known as the Jourdan-Delbrel law, was applied until 1818, with however an amendment in 1804 to introduce the drawing of lots and authorize replacement. Each canton had to provide a certain quota of men, about 30 to 35% of the conscripts, chosen by lot. The law also allows the wealthiest to negotiate a sum before a notary to pay a replacement who was doing military service in place of the conscript.

Despite these laws, as war became continual over much of Europe, recruitment became more and more difficult, replacement more and more expensive, and conscription more and more unpopular.

In 1815, conscription was abolished and the Napoleonic army was disbanded. But as the number of staff was insufficient, Gouvion Saint-Cyr passed a law in 1818 that instituted a six-year service to which young people who had drawn a wrong number had to comply. After 6 years of service, conscripts were released but transferred to veterans (equivalent to the reserve according to the current term). Between 1815 and 1870, the mass of French soldiers was made up of conscripts who had drawn a wrong number, replacements and volunteer enlistments.

In 1855, the paid exemption replaced replacement. But in 1868, to cope with the decline in the number of troops and the professionalization of the army, the law abolished the exemption and reinstated the replacement.

It was in this context of recruitment that France declared war on Prussia on 19 July 1870. This conflict pitted France against a coalition of German states led by Prussia. The conflict ended on 28 January 1871 with the signing of an armistice by which the German states proclaimed a German Empire which annexed Alsace and Lorraine.

The law of 27 July 1872 proclaimed the principle of personal military service, replacement was abolished but the drawing of lots was maintained. Half of the contingent must complete five years of active service, the other half one year. As in previous laws, many exceptions are provided for teachers, ministers of religion or certain graduates, for example.

It was not until 1905 that recruitment by drawing lots and possible replacement disappeared. The law of 21 March 1905 established for the first time the principle of compulsory, equal and universal military service as it was known until 1998, the year in which the Defence and Citizenship Day was created, which gave young men and women between the ages of 16 and 25 information on their rights and duties as citizens, than on the functioning of the institutions.

10. from 1850 to 1900

Honoré Cestia

During the period 1850-1900 the Cestia were present on the planet in the following regions: Argentina, Uruguay, the United States, and in France mainly in Bigorre.

I have been able to count more than 200 people born with this surname between 1850 and 1900. This is much more than during the last 50 years in France.

Honoré Cestia

Honoré Cestia was born in 1857 in the small village of Louit, which at the time had about 280 inhabitants. Vines, wheat and corn are grown there. Cattle are used for transport and land work. It is a poor village of about forty houses, most of which are more than 200 years old.

Honoré's father, Philippe, was nearly 43 years old at the time of his son's birth. Honoré's mother, Madeleine [59] from Coussan, located south of Louit, a few kilometers away, was not yet 21 years old. A few years after Honoré's birth, his brother Auguste Sylvain arrived in 1864.

The Sentubery

Three kilometres north of Louit lives in the village of Castera-Lou, the Sentubery family. A family whose influence would be decisive, as we will see below. In 1829 Dominique Sentubery, originally from Oleac-Débat, four kilometres south of Louit, after his marriage to Simone Sénac de Castéra-Lou settled in his native village. Between 1830 and 1846, there were six children, the three youngest, Jean and his sisters, Marie and Victorine, who migrated to Uruguay in 1857. Jean was 19 years old at the time and his sisters were 15 and 11 years old.

Some time later, Jean was joined by his first cousin from Oléac-Debat, Jean-Marie, known as *"the One-Eyed"*, and his first cousin Jeanne-Marie.

In 1860, at the age of 22, Jean Sentubery, a shoemaker by trade, founded the Zapatería (shoe store) in Montevideo *"The Golden Ball"*, (La boule d'Or) Rincón y Juncal street.

In 1864 there was the marriage of Marie (22 years old), Jean's sister, who married Jean Jules Mothe of a family originally from France. A year after the wedding, Victorine Mothe was born.

---

59 Magdelaine on her birth certificate. But we also find on some documents the spelling Madelaine.

Then in 1871, after the birth of their first child, Jean Sentubery married his first cousin Jeanne Marie, the mother of his child.

Thus, in Montevideo, a cosmopolitan city with a large population of French origin, there was in 1876 a large Sentubery family from a village very close to Louit where Jean Sentubery's property adjoined that of Abraham Dortignac the uncle of Madeleine Dortignac, the mother of Honoré.

Uruguay

The Oriental Republic of Uruguay or Uruguay is the smallest country in South America. It has an area equal to a third of that of France. Uruguay is located between 30° and 35° south latitude, south of Brazil, and east of Argentina, from which it is separated

by the Uruguay River which gave it its name. Its territory is essentially made up of plains crossed by numerous rivers, a geographical feature favourable to livestock farming.

Spanish colonization of the Rio de la Plata region began60 in the 16th century. The indigenous peoples violently opposed this invasion. Before Uruguay's independence in 1828, there were many conflicts between the Spanish and the Portuguese, but also between the English and the French and the Spanish. The weakening of Spain in 1810 and the rivalry between Buenos Aires and Montevideo gave rise to an aspiration for independence in Uruguay. It took many violent confrontations between the Argentinian, Uruguayan, Spanish, Portuguese, and Brazilian peoples, forging and unwinding alliances as opportunities arose, to culminate in the adoption of the

---

60 The "Río de la Plata" is the estuary created by the Río Paraná and the Río Uruguay. To the south of the estuary is Argentina, to the north Uruguay.

first Uruguayan constitution on July 18, 1830.

From that date until the beginning of the 20th century, Uruguay experienced numerous conflicts with neighbouring countries. At the same time, many immigrants, especially Europeans, came to settle in Uruguay. During the Great War between Uruguay and Argentina at the hands of the dictator Rosas, the French made up more than half of the city's foreign population. In 1843, in the midst of the siege of Montevideo, the French behaved like heroes to defend the city against the Argentine attackers. This episode welded the Franco-Uruguayan friendship together for a long time.

From 1850 onwards, Uruguay experienced a strong growth in its population due[61] to a much more diversified immigration. At the end of the 19th century, Montevideo had a large foreign population from Italy, Spain, Brazil, and Argentina. Uruguayan institutions have fostered the integration of these populations, allowing this country to build itself on the cultural contributions of Spain, France, Italy, Germany, England and the United States.

Honoré migre in Uruguay

Around 1876, Honoré migrated to Uruguay. He was the eldest and his mother was a widow, which, under article 17 of the law of 27 July 1872, exempted him from military service. This legislative provision is intended for the son to stay with his mother to help him, which is not the choice of Honoré and his mother. Honoré, no doubt in agreement with his mother, decides to leave for Uruguay.

This choice to leave is probably dictated by multiple motivations. It seems clear that the presence in this country of many French people was an important factor, especially since these French people present in Montevideo were not all unknown. When he left for Montevideo, Honoré met up with the Sentuberys, acquaintances and neighbours from his native village.

In Dours, located 2 km from Louit, the brothers Bernard and Jacques Cestia, from a family of shoemakers, left for Montevideo before they were 20 years old to escape military enlistment.

What can we also say about Jean Sentubery's visit to Oléac-Debat in 1875. He could have organised his succession in Montevideo and *"negotiate"* with Madeleine the marriage of his niece to Honoré ... Anything is possible, at that time parents were still very influential...

Finally, it was known in Louit that those who returned from Uruguay generally returned richer than they had left... In Louit the Cestia did not live miserably. Philippe

---

[61] The Uruguayan population grew from 100,000 inhabitants in 1850, probably a third of whom were French, to nearly one million in 1908.

Cestia Honoré's father was at the time of his marriage a well-to-do man. [62]. He had left young, penniless, for Guadeloupe, and had returned with an income. Is it a lure of profit or a desire to follow in his father's footsteps? I'll let you choose.

Thus Madeleine made Honoré leave and kept her youngest son Auguste Sylvain with her. However, Honoré was the eldest, and therefore the one who should have taken over the farm, since in 1876 his father had died. In Bigorre at that time, the birthright, although abolished by the French Revolution, was still very much present in usage. Usually, the youngest were sent away to leave the elders to watch over the inheritance.

Honoré probably left Louit in 1876 or early 1877. He does not set off on an adventure, to conquer the new world, risking his life on a dangerous journey. No, he simply took the boat to Bordeaux to, after a little more than 10 days at sea, meet up with compatriots, acquaintances who formed a family and business clan in Montevideo, a network as we would say today.

Victorine Mothe

In particular, he met Jean Sentubery who was barely 39 years old at the time, but had already done well, and was at the head of a shoe business, a farm and owned several investment properties. Thus made his fortune, Jean Sentubery thought of returning to France. It is for this purpose that he has brought his nephew Dominique Dupont.

When he arrived in Montevideo, Honoré Cestia probably had no difficulty in finding enough to live on; he probably worked for the Sentuberys. And this is how he met his future wife Victorine Mothe, whose mother was a Sentubery.

---

62 Philippe Cestia's marriage contract indicates that the future husband would build up the sum of 20,000 francs, money, bonds, securities, investments, in addition to 1,000 francs. This represents more than 30 years of an average annual salary at the time. Today, 30 years of the minimum wage represents about €480,000.

Dupont x Meyranx

As for Dominique Dupont, Jean Sentubery's nephew, who had just arrived in Montevideo, he married Eugénie Meyranx, the daughter of Eugène Meyranx originally from the Landes, he arrived in Montevideo in 1867 with his wife and children. Eugène Meyranx was a carpenter like his father and grandfather. He created a carpentry company and a sawmill that participated in the construction of the « *Government House* » [63]. He also built *"Folly"* in the beautiful Prado and *"The Union"* where he settles. He also participated in the construction of several French-style villas in Arcachon on the « *Rambla de Pocitos* » a quarter of Montevideo.

On June 16, 1886, the newspaper *"El Dia"*, for which it was the first issue, published an advertisement announcing the transfer of Jean Sentubery's business to his nephews. It is Dominique Dupont married to Eugénie Meyranx and Honoré Cestia his nephew by marriage married to Victorine Mothe. And this is how Jean Sentubery was able to retire in France in his native village.

The shoe trade is doing well, no doubt driven by the sharp increase in the immigrant population with high purchasing power. The nephews and nieces live in two apartments above the store. Their families grew (see next chapter).

Returning home
Shortly after his return to France in 1899, Honoré Cestia married Anna a 17-year-old girl, he was 44 years old ... An unusual age difference that must have surprised many... including, I know, his son Felix and his wife Julie, the same age as his mother-in-law. Yet his father had also married a woman much younger than him. Five years later, André was born, whose youngest of his half-brothers Jules was 14 years old at the time, and the oldest Felix was almost 20 years old. Anna was in fragile health. She died at the age of 40 in 1925. The same year, Honoré lost his mother, who was 88 years old. Thus Honoré found himself alone with his 18-year-old son André.

---

63 A prestigious residence in Buenos Aires that is now one of the tourist attractions of this city.

> **A social work in Nay**
>
> The increase in the working population, the poverty of social protection and living conditions will question at length the three Abbé Dupont who will embark at the end of the nineteenth century on a remarkable great social work. They first opened a classical educational establishment in the middle of the century, then from 1865 in their family estate in Mouliérats, a Saint-Joseph hospice that could accommodate 14 people.
>
> From 1868, with the purchase of the Palengat estate (now the Collège et Lycée Saint-Joseph), they began their great architectural work. The first building was that of the Dominican Convent (now the Monastery of the Beatitudes), then the Institution Saint-Joseph intended for the education of young boys and especially the renovation and reconstruction of the Saint-Joseph hospice from 1892.
>
> Very well designed, it subscribes to the needs of hygiene and morality. It is also equipped to receive accident victims.
>
> (Official website of the city of Nay)

Honoré was, according to the testimonies collected, of a calm and peaceful nature; his nickname was a patois word meaning *"beetle."*

In 1934, two months after the death of his father, André married Graziella Dupont. André lived on the family farm in Louit. He was mobilized during the Second World War. He died for France in Vienne-le-Château on 11 June 1940.

Auguste Sylvain Cestia

Unlike his older brother, Auguste Sylvain Cestia is not eligible for a national service exemption. At the age of 20 in 1884, during the census, he drew the number 32, a number unfortunately far too weak to escape the 5-year service. Indeed, the law of 1872 provided that half of the contingent, chosen by lot, had to complete five years of active service, the other one year. Auguste Sylvain Cestia is therefore convened on 30 December 1885 for the revision council which was to rule on his fitness to be a soldier. But on December 30, 1885, he was already far away. He is in Montevideo, Uruguay where he has joined his brother Honoré. He is therefore declared insubordinate and faces a sentence of 1 month to one year in prison.

Auguste Sylvain chose to flee to avoid conscription, probably encouraged by his mother who cherishes her children more than anything, and for whom a future as a soldier for her son for 5 years and the risk of being engaged in a new war probably seems unbearable.

Madeleine Dortignac Auguste Sylvain's mother was born in 1838. She has the memory of these incessant wars of France since 1852. The Emperor Napoleon III, Louis-Napoleon Bonaparte fought in 1853-1856 in the Black Sea, in 1856-1860 in China, in 1859-1862 in Cochinchina (Vietnam), in 1859 in Lombardy and Veneto, in 1861 in Mexico, in 1866 in Korea, and in 1870 in Germany, a war that the Republic continued. It is easy to imagine that the victories of the Emperor of the French or of the Republic matters little to Madeleine Dortignac.

For her sons, it was therefore the war that Madeleine Dortignac, widow Cestia, feared the most, she who, much later, in 1914, trembled for her grandson Jules.

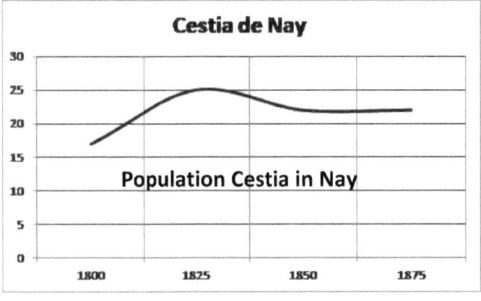

Auguste Sylvain did not stay in Montevideo, he settled in Buenos Aires in Argentina where many French migrants lived. He did not have the same success as his brother, he died at the age of 33 without ever having seen his native village again.

The Cestia in Nay

Nay is a small town in the Pyrénées-Atlantiques

In Nay the Cestia are also called Cestiaa or Sestiaa. This is surprising, but it is in line with the local usage of doubling the terminal vowel!

The Cestia, Sestiaa, Sestia, Cestiaa and Cestia were present in Nay during the period 1850 to 1900. They are the children, grandchildren or great-grandchildren of Pierre Sestiaa (1783-1844), by Jean Pierre Sestiaa (1780-1855), of Jean Sestia (1787-1849), and Jean Paul Sestiaa (1802-1874)). Pierre, Jean Pierre, Jean and Jean Paul, their ancestors, are first cousins.

Thus, at the end of the nineteenth century, we can say that the Cestia de Nay family is a large family. They are workers, 50% of them working in the textile industry, but 35% are craftsmen or shopkeepers and 15% are in the woodworking trades, another important industry in Nay.

The Cestia de Nay participated in the increase of the working population of Nay, whose poor social protection and harsh living conditions questioned the three Abbés Dupont.

The Cestia in Dordogne and Gironde

Bordeaux was, in the period 1850-1900, an attractive city because of its important seaport.

It was there that François Cestia and his companion Marie Cécile Eugénie settled around 1870 for a while on their return from Guadeloupe before returning permanently to the native village of Lescurry.

It was also the home of Charles Hippolyte who, at birth, was registered under the name of his mother, Françoise Jeanne Guinle, then recognized by his father when he married the child's mother.

But Bordeaux is also linked by waterways that promote trade with the interior of the territory: the Dordogne connects Bordeaux to Libourne, and to Bergerac. Inland waterway transport was an important activity on the Dordogne in the middle of the nineteenth century.

This is how Bernard Cestia, born in Vic-en-Bigorre from a family of masons, married in 1825 Marthe Durive from a family of boatmen. The family name leads us to presume that inland waterway fishing is a long tradition of this family.

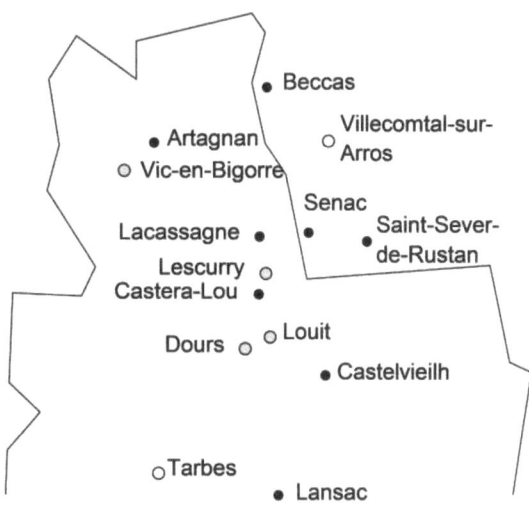

Bernard and Marthe lived in Bergerac where they had their first three children, then in Libourne where they had four more children. Two of them, Charles Jean and Eugène, settled there. Charles Jean married there but died immediately after his marriage. Eugene, his brother, then married the widow and they had a child whom they named Charles Jean after the deceased brother.

The Cestia in Bigorre and Astarac

This overview of the Cestia in the second half of the nineteenth century shows us that the settlement in a neighbouring village was often done on the occasion of a marriage with a girl from another village. These are migrations to a village very close to a few kilometres.

The departure from Lescurry, where the land is thankless, is preferably made to villages with more generous agriculture, Castera-Lou, Lacassagne or Sénac. [64].

There is also a movement of rural exodus. The migration in Bigorre to the city, the rural exodus of the Cestia, mainly benefited Vic-en-Bigorre much more than Tarbes, the large city, whose population tripled in the nineteenth century.

According to the historian Georges Dupeux [], this migration is65 improperly called *"rural exodus",* because it concerns the departure of a surplus of population that does not lead to the abandonment of the rural territory, in this case for the Cestia the village of Lescurry.

---

64 According to the information found in the municipal monographs of 1887 drawn up by the teachers.

65 Georges Dupeux, "La société française 1789-1970", 1972, Armand Colin, p 21

Concerning the city of Lyon and the countryside, Mr. Garden [66] says "It constantly sends the surplus of its population to the city, it is a permanent reservoir from which the city draws with growing needs", to which Gabriel Audisio replies [67]"What is true of Lyon applies to all urban organizations", and this is understandable, also true for Vic-en-Bigorre, even if, as we will see later, the latter is the object of a migratory attraction with a much older origin.

It was thus, through migration, that the surname Cestia spread in Bigorre between 1850 and 1900. Population movements are often motivated by the search for better land to cultivate.

The name of the former county of Bigorre is still very much used in the department of Hautes-Pyrénées where it becomes almost the way to designate the department, although it was smaller than the department created in 1790. On the other hand, in the north, the former territory of the County of Astarac no longer has the same notoriety. This former territory is located both in the north of the current department of Hautes-Pyrénées and, for the most part, in the present-day Gers.

The Cestia in the Hautes-Pyrénées

At the end of the nineteenth century, there were many Cestia in the Hautes-Pyrénées and in the south of the Gers. They are mainly present in Vic-en-Bigorre, Lescurry, Dours and Louit. But they are also present in many other villages: Beccas, Lansac, Artagnan, Castelvieilh, Castera-Lou, Lacassagne, Saint-Sever-de-Rustan, and Sénac.

Vic-en-Bigorre

In Vic-en-Bigorre, between 1850 and 1900, we find Jean Cestia butcher, and Antoinette Dauriac, his wife, who had nine children, the eldest of whom lived for some time in Guadeloupe. Jean is originally from Beccas in the Gers where his father was *"ploughman"*. He is a Coutillou from a family of Lescurry.

Jean Bertrand's brother is also a butcher, so we can think that the two brothers worked together.

We know that until the nineteenth century, *"ploughman"* referred to the status of the peasant who owned the land he cultivated and at least one team, horse or pair of oxen, and plough.

Also living in Vic Jean Cestia and his wife Dominiquette Setze. He was a daily farmer, that is to say a simple labourer, also called a labourer, from a family also from Lescurry.

---

66 Garden, "Lyon and the Lyonnais in the Eighteenth Century", 1970.
67 Gabriel Audisio, "Des paysans XVème-XIXème siècle", 1993, p 342

Alexandre Cestia, known as Darric, originally from Lescurry, and his wife from Vic had five children in Vic. Alexandre was, in this village, a sharecropper of the estate of St Aunis (known as the castle) owned by the Lataste family, then a ploughman and owner.

In Vic we also have Joseph Cestia originally from Lescurry, servant at the castle of St Aunis and farmer, and his wife Jeanne Marie Ader who have two children.

Antoine Cestia, a mason from a family from Louit who came to settle in Vic, has, with Anne Bire, five children including Bernard He left for Bergerac after his marriage.

Lescurry

At the end of this century, Lescurry was not an attractive village, its population was in sharp decline. In 1887 the teacher wrote about his village: *"The soil of Lescurry, which is not the best, requires a lot of care and fertilizer."* (Municipal monograph of teachers)

In 1900, there were only eight inhabitants of Lescurry bearing the surname Cestia, whereas there were twenty in 1850.

In this village of less than 300 inhabitants, many of the Cestia who live there have often been established for several generations. With rare exceptions, they do not come from the surrounding villages. Conversely, some will settle in neighbouring villages at the time of their marriage.

Dours

Jean Cestia (1792-1867) farmer in Dours was born of an unknown father and Jeanne Marie Sestia de Dours. He is a medalist of *"Saint Helena"*. The Saint Helena medal, created by Napoleon III, rewards the 405,000 soldiers still alive in 1857, who fought alongside Napoleon 1st during the wars of 1792-1815.

Of the 4 Cestia families settled in Dours, only two Cestia married outside their village.

Municipal monograph of primary school teachers

In 1886, the city of Toulouse decided to organise, from 15 May to 15 October 1887, an "International Exhibition under the patronage of the State". The Toulouse City Hall, which wanted to set up a large-scale Exhibition, asked the Rector of the Academy to dedicate a room to teaching. The proposal is to present "all the documents that make it possible to ascertain the current state of public education in the Academy of Toulouse and to compare it with what it was ten years ago."

Following this request, the inspector of the Academy of Tarbes sent the following request to the teachers of the Hautes-Pyrénées on 11 January 1887:

"All tenured teachers without exception, and female teachers directing mixed schools, must send to the Academic Inspectorate the monograph of their commune drawn up, as far as possible, according to the following indications, which do not exclude the new developments that the authors would like to give

In Dours, Paul Felix married after his return from the 1870-1871 war against Germany.

Louit.

In Louit there were in 1850 the families of the three brothers Cestia, Philippe, Martial and Jean, i.e., with their children and their wives, 15 people. In 1900, only Madame Madeleine Cestia, née Dortignac, mother of Honoré Cestia, remained.

Beccas

Arnaud Cestia was born in Beccas and his sister Marie, son and daughter of Jean, a ploughman. Arnaud left Beccas and settled in Malabat, near Beccas in the Gers. He became mayor and his son Jean-Baptiste, a magistrate, was named Knight of the Legion of Honour on 9 August 1854.

But this appointment intrigues some, because the father, Arnaud, is Sestia while the son, Jean-Baptiste President of the Court of Tarbes and member of the General Council, is Cestia ... which led the mayor of Malabat, to regularize the file, to sign the following declaration:

« ... the father signed his name with an S, while the son always wrote his name with a C, as is to our personal knowledge, and this is also established by numerous acts deposited in the archives of the present municipality that the late Mr. Cestia senior signed in his capacity as mayor and by other acts signed by the said Mr. Cestia junior as a member of the municipal council and otherwise. »

Biography of Jean Adnet extracted from the dictionary of French parliamentarians from 1789 to 1889 (A. Robert and G. Cougny)

... after practising for some time as a lawyer, entered the magistracy.

During the elections for the National Assembly, on February 8, 1871, he was brought to the department of Hautes-Pyrénées on a list in which M. Thiers appeared, and elected.

He first sat on the centre right, and took a decisive part in the discussion of the famous Rivet proposal (session of 12 August 1871). Scarcely had M. Rivet asked that M. Thiers, the head of the executive power, be conferred the title of President of the Republic, and that his powers be extended for three years, when M. Adnet succeeded him on the rostrum to table a counter-proposal for the purpose of confirming purely and simply to M. Thiers the powers which the Assembly had conferred on him at Bordeaux. Very favourably received by the right, the Adnet proposal, like the other, obtained an emergency vote, but was not adopted

Mr. Adnet did not intervene in any other important debate in the Assembly.

In the senatorial elections of January 30, 1876, Mr. Adnet was elected. He sat on the right of the Senate,

Mr. Adnet, who was not re-elected at the triennial renewal of January 2, 1882, has returned to private life.

As for John the Baptist's daughter, Izaure Cestia, she married Jean Joseph Marie Eugène Adnet (1822-1900) French politician, deputy and senator who sat on the right in the hemicycle from 1871 to 1882.

Marie, Jean Cestia's daughter, left Beccas to settle in Vic-en-Bigorre after her marriage to Jean Despalanques, merchant in Pointe-à-Pitre in Guadeloupe, founder of the trading company Despalanques et Cie

Lansac
It was in Lansac that Jean Sestian was born in 1789 who married Domenge Daubes. Their son named Jean Sestia has 6 children all born in Lansac. The eldest of the boys was exempted from the army because he was *"eldest son of a widow"*. Thus, in 1860, there were, in Lansac, 8 descendants of Jean Sestian, who died in 1854, all of whom were called Sestia.

Other villages
Cestia also settled in several other villages: in Artagnan Vincent Cestia farmer from Louit, in Castelvieilh Paul Hyppolite Cestia farmer from Dours, in Castera-Lou Louis Cestia farmer from Lescurry. In Lacassagne there was also in 1843 the marriage of Jean-Marie Cestia by Lescurry with Dominiquette Roques de Lacassagne. Then in 1846 that of Antoine Cestia of Sénac with Domenge Dulac. Bernarde Cestia de Louit married in Saint-Sever-de-Rustan. Jean Cestian Coubé de Lescurry married in Sénac in 1786 to Marguerite Cougot de Sénac who bore him 4 children, 2 girls, then 2 boys. The first of the boys won a medal in St. Helena. On his return from the military campaign, he settled in Sénac. The second married Dours.

The Cestia in the Americas

Argentina
Bernard Cestia is a carpenter. He was born in 1814 in Nay, where his father was born in the *"laneficier"* trade or wool trade. In 1850, he moved to Vic-en-Bigorre to prepare for his departure to Argentina. He started a family in Buenos Aires where his two children, Adela Maria and Catalina, were born in 1855 and 1859.

In Dours, located 2 km from Louit, the brothers Bernard and Jacques Cestia, from a family of shoemakers, both left for Montevideo at the age of 20, around 1860 for the former and 1866 for the latter. Bernard worked there as a café owner and then as a baker. He married for the first time, but quickly became a widower. He then settled in Buenos Aires where he married his first cousin Dorothée Cestia at the age of 40, 26 years old, born in Castelvieilh to a family also from Dours.

Joseph Cestia (1847-1871) was born in Pujo (near Vic) to a family originally from Vic-en-Bigorre. At the age of 19 (1866), before being summoned for the revision board, he migrated to Buenos Aires. Around 1895 he was joined by his sister Marie and his brother-in-law Joseph Dedieu.

Joseph Dedieu is originally from Vic. He married Marie Cestia also from Vic-en-Bigorre. They settled in Tarbes where he was a jeweller. In 1881, their son Michel Georges was born. It was after the birth of their child that the family migrated to Buenos Aires in 1895.

Jean Cestia was born in 1813 in Lescurry into a family originally from this village. He married in 1843 in Lacassagne where his son Dominique was born. He then settled between 1860 and 1870 in Buenos Aires. He finally returned to Lacassagne around 1872.

Louisiana

Jean Alphé Cestia (1834-1860)) migrated to Louisiana at a very young age of 14 (1848). One can think that his parents did not let him leave Vic-en-Bigorre, his hometown, alone. It was probably accompanied by a relative or friend that he arrived in America where he met Bertrand Cestia also from Vic. He did not stay in New Orleans but settled in Abbeville where he married Marie Zulma Fontelieux who is 16 years old, he is 22. Three years after his marriage and after the birth of his son Alexander and daughter Marie Laura, he died at the age of 25. His wife Marie Zulma then moved to Vermillion and then 9 years later to New Iberia where she died at the age of 37 (1877). Alexander had many children.

The Cestia in Italy

I don't know anything about the Cestia in Italy, but I'll tell you everything... The Cestia in Italy are part of the 12% of files for which my research could not lead to a satisfactory conclusion. So I'm giving you what I know like the one whose boat is going to sink, and who throws a bottle into the sea with a message inside that he hopes to be read someday somewhere.

Fortunato Cestius

Fortunato Cestius was born at the end of the nineteenth century in Rome via San Felice Circeo (12 km from the center of Rome). When in the summer of 1907, he embarked in Naples aboard the Cretic bound for America, he lived with his mother in the house where he was born. He arrived in New York on July 27, 1907 with 12 dollars in his pocket. He is a farm worker, single and can neither read nor write. He is to be reunited with his brother-in-law in the United States, J. Antonia Armento Payton. The doctor H McMaste, who examined him, found him in robust.

Sérafina Cestia

Sérafina Cestia, born around 1875 in Alcara li fusi in Sicily, landed in New York on September 16, 1910 to be reunited with her brother. She comes from Palermo in Sicily. She can neither read nor write. She has $15 dollars in her pocket.

C Cestia

C Cestia was born in 1854 in Italy. He landed in New York in 1890 aboard the *"La Normandie"*

Giuseppe Cestia
Giuseppe Cestia was Italian, born around 1876. He comes from Tusa, located between Messina and Palermo. He travelled on the Vancouver. He is a sailor. He could neither read nor write. He arrived in Boston in 1903.

John Cestius
Giovanni Cestia is Italian. He does not know how to write his name, which is transcribed phonetically into Spanish. Thus, when he settled and married Rosa Braidoti in Argentina, he became Juan Ceschia. Between 1885 and 1905, they had 9 children.

Maria Cestia
Maria Cestia was born in Italy around 1826. At the age of 72, on April 22, 1898, she landed in New York from Genoa.

11. The Cestia in France in the twentieth century

The figures presented below are those of INSEE. They concern the surnames Cestia, Sestia and Sestiaa. There was both a low number of births and a sharp decrease in births with these surnames in France over the period 1891-1990.

By way of comparison, it is interesting to note that the same INSEE statistics count, over the period 1891-1915 alone, 19,231 births and 10,789 for the Duponts.

Births in France by department from 1891 to 1990

1891-1915		Cestia	Sestia	Sestiaa	Total
Bouches-du-Rhône	13	2			2
Gers	32	2			2
Gironde	33	3			3
Pyrénées-Atlantiques	64			7	7
Hautes-Pyrénées	65	1	2		3
Total		8	2	7	17

1916-1940		Cestius	Sestia	Sestiaa	Total
Haute-Garonne	31			2	2
Gironde	33	5			5
Pyrénées-Atlantiques	64			6	6
Hautes-Pyrénées	65	7	2		9
Total		12	2	8	22

1941-1965		Cestius	Sestia	Sestiaa	Total
Gard	30	2			2
Gironde	33	5			5
Hérault	34	1			1
Marl	51	2			2
Pyrénées-Atlantiques	64			7	7
Hautes-Pyrénées	65	5	1		6
Yonne	89	1			1
Total		16	1	7	24

1966-1990		Cestius	Sestia	Sestiaa	Total
Gironde	33	2			2

		Cestius	Sestia	Sestiaa	Total
Marl	51	2			2
Pyrénées-Atlantiques	64			4	4
Hautes-Pyrénées	65	1			1
Hauts-de-Seine	92	4			4
Total		9		4	13

1891-1990		Cestius	Sestia	Sestiaa	Total
Bouches-du-Rhône	13	2			2
Gard	30	2			
Haute-Garonne	31			2	
Gers	32	2			2
Gironde	33	15			15
Hérault	34	1			
Marl	51	4			
Pyrénées-Atlantiques	64			24	24
Hautes-Pyrénées	65	14	5		19
Yonne	89	1			
Hauts-de-Seine	92	4			
Total		45	5	26	76

12. from 1900 to 1946 Felix Cestia

When the three Cestia brothers arrived in Bordeaux, they left everything behind, their childhood, their country. They were leaving Felipe, ÉmilioJulio to become PhilippeEmile and Jules, three young immigrants.

Their boat had left the Rio de la Plata almost two weeks ago. He had left Buenos Aires, then stopped at Montevideo. It was there that they had embarked with their father and their paternal grandmother who, a short time before, had made the trip in the other direction when she learned of the widowhood of her son Honoré and the death of her last child Victor. The *"Family legend"*, by which I mean facts that were reported to me orally but that I have not been able to verify, says that she would have cheated on her age to be able to make the crossing.

The three young people had only their maternal grandparents in Montevideo, they only knew from photos this grandmother Madeleine who, one fine day, arrived from France to console them for the sorrow they felt both at the loss of their mother who died in 1899 during the birth of her son Victor, but also for the sorrow they felt at the

accidental death of Victor in his first year. It was this last misfortune that decided the grandmother Madeleine Marthe Dortignac to pick up her son and three grandchildren.

Grandmother Madeleine had come to help her son with his move. So they left Montevideo and the comfortable life in a beautiful apartment located above the shoe store managed by their father and Domingo Dupont their mother's first cousin. They thus left their cousins Dupont, Domingo and his wife Eugénie and their three children, who were also their next-door neighbours. There was Eugenio, the same age as Felipe, the Potota and Juan Carlos the last, who was only a few years old but already showed his energetic character.

Back in France, Honoré and his three children settled only temporarily on the family farm in Louit; but after almost twenty years in Montevideo, he finally preferred to live in Aureilhan, closer to the city of Tarbes, where his children could be more conveniently educated. And then his Uruguayan epic had given him a certain material ease, [68] he was now a rentier. So he bought a car and so Louit, located about 8 kilometers away, became much closer.

The eldest of the three children, my grandfather, was of Uruguayan nationality because his father had not taken the necessary steps to ensure that he also had French nationality when he was born. His first name was Felipe, which became Philippe on official French documents. But in fact everyone called him Felix. A name frequently used in the Rio de la Plata. The close sound of Felipe probably explains the use of this other name. When he arrived in France around 1900, he was just 14 years old. Before him, his parents had a son Juan probably died very young.

Then there was Emile who was two years younger than Felix, then Jules who arrived 4 years later.

In Uruguay with their mother, who was an *"Oriental"* [69] name by which the inhabitants of the Oriental Republic of Uruguay were designated, they spoke Spanish and with their father French.

Felix, once he graduated from the Ecole Supérieure de Commerce de Bordeaux, found a job at the Uruguayan consulate in Marseille. He settled in the *Hôtel des deux*

---

68 In 1902, the marriage contract between Honoré Cestia and Anna Villa mentions Honoré's assets in securities and real estate of 50,000 Francs, or about €135,000 in 2016, which represents about 27 years of the average annual salary of a worker in 1900. Today, 27 years of annual minimum wage are about €380,000.

69 Victorine Mothe, the mother of Felix, Emile and Jules, had dual French and Uruguayan nationality.

mondes. There he met his future wife Julie Laurens, the daughter of the owner from Pélissanne. He married her in 1912.

Julie introduced Emile, her future brother-in-law; to an acquaintance of Pélissanne, Fernande Gauthier. The following year, in 1913, Emile married Fernande, who came from a bourgeois family in Pélissanne.

And so it was that Emile became a postmaster in Salon de Provence, a few kilometres from Pélissanne.

Emile and Felix loved the theatre, music and the arts. Fernande's sister played the piano skilfully and with talent. This well-to-do youth was enjoying these few years of happiness.

But the cursed war came. Felix, who was planning a trip to Montevideo, had to give it up. Jules, who was in the army when Germany declared war on France, was the first to be mobilized (August 1914). In September he was in combat.

Felix Cestia

In August 1914, Felix who was a Uruguayan escaped the mobilization.

Continuing his career at the Uruguayan consulate in Marseille, where he had returned at the end of his studies in 1912, he became chancellor, then on 17 July 1925 he was appointed vice-consul of Uruguay in Marseille.

1925 Appointment of Felipe Cestia as Uruguayan Vice Consul in Marseille

The President of the Eastern Republic of Uruguay informs that, wishing to increase relations and maintain the necessary communication between this Republic and that of France, he has appointed Citizen Felipe Cestia to assume the office of Vice-Consul in Marseilles.

Consequently, it requests the Government of France to allow Mr. Felipe Cestia to freely exercise the functions of Vice-Consul with the prerogatives and exemptions corresponding to his rank and function.

I am sending this certificate, stamped with the stamp of the Arms of the Republic and authenticated by the Minister Secretary of State of the Department of Foreign Affairs, to Montevideo on the seventeenth day of July, one thousand nine hundred and twenty-five.

In parallel with his duties as a diplomat, Felix had a liberal activity as an insurance agent which, like his duties as a diplomat, he carried out in the offices that occupied part of his apartment at 37, rue Estelle in Marseille.

After Maurice's birth in 1913, in the civil registry « *Mauricio Mario Honorato*», said during his early years *"Mimi"*, 2 years later Chiquita Said *"Tita"*, then again 4 years later Emile said *"Snowy"*

Holidays were often spent with the family

in Louit (Hautes-Pyrénées). The journey to reach Aureilhan's uncle and aunt, Jules and Thérèse, was done by bike, sometimes with the young cousin on the bike, with or without falls... Uncle Jules, on the other hand, made the trips with the cart and the mare.

But Felix and Julie's happiness doesn't last long. In 1928, Chiquita was killed by tuberculosis, when she was only 12 years old.

In 1934, it was a holiday in Italy, from July 14 to August 22, probably at the home of a distant cousin of Julie's, the

Marquise Andrée del Rangoni Castel Crescente ... 1934 was also the year in which Maurice, who was no longer called "Mimi", signed a declaration on 3 January with his parents, reserved for minors over 16 years of age, in which he applied for French nationality, which was granted to him on 16 March 1934. [70]

And then in 1936, the fatality of the disease once again struck the family with the death of Milou, also affected by tuberculosis at the age of 16.

In June 1937, Maurice finished his engineering studies in Grenoble. Felix and Julie then find themselves alone in Marseille.

And again the war came, Maurice who, before he came of age, had decided to be French, was mobilized. He fought from 2 September 1939 to 25 June 1940 on the Rhobach Plateau, in the Basses-Vosges and in the Somme, which earned him two citations in the order of the Regiment and the Croix de Guerre (2 bronze stars).

In April 1942, France was occupied by the Germans. During the World War, Uruguay remained neutral. However, an incident between the British and a military vessel off the coast of Montevideo led Germany to suspend diplomatic relations with Uruguay on 25 January 1942.

This is why Felix cannot obtain permission to travel to the Paris region to attend his son's wedding. Only Julie, his wife, who is French, obtained the authorization. It was only in September that Felix was able to meet his daughter-in-law in Alès in the Gard.

A little later in 1943, the difficult relations between Germany and Uruguay led to new problems. The Germans let Felix know that he had a choice between going to Uruguay or going to Spain, where Franco agreed to take him in. He opted for Spain. He was immediately escorted back to the border by two German officers. For several long months, he was unable to communicate with his family. He then managed to smuggle mail through Switzerland.

In Barcelona he has the rank of diplomat. The *"family legend"* tells that during a hunting trip to which he had been invited by Franco, the latter confided in him about the difficulty of solitude that one feels in power... Personally I have always found it funny that a dictator feels alone and suffers from it... It is also said that Jules, about this hunting trip, said to his brother Felix, *"Fortunately they didn't give you a gun, because clever as you are, you could have killed Franco!"*

At the end of the war, many Spanish republicans who had taken refuge in France hoped to take power in Spain, but did not find the international support they had hoped for. Churchill declared in May 1944 *"The internal political problems in Spain are the business of the Spaniards themselves"*

---

70 In application of the law of 10 August 1927.

It was in this context that on 26 January 1946 the French government decided to close the border with Spain from 1 March 1946.

Despite this difficult political context, Felix was able to return to France from 5 May 1945 to 6 June 1945 for a short stay.

On January 28, 1946, before the border was closed, *"Lili"*, Felix's wife, was allowed to join him in Barcelona. But they were not able to return to France until October 1946.

Felix then resumed his duties as Vice-Consul and Chancellor of the Uruguayan Consulate in Marseille.

"Lili" for some, *"Mamy"* for others, has never really recovered from the mourning of her children and her husband who left 22 years before her at the age of 66. A long time later, when she recalled these painful memories, tears came to her eyes, and then there were also her husband's three years of exile that had stolen part of her life.

> Uruguay remained neutral in both world wars. It broke off diplomatic relations with Germany on 7 October 1914, but did not join the 23 sovereign states that declared war on Germany. Uruguay remained neutral during the outbreak of the Second World War despite international pressure to join the allies. But on January 25, 1942, Uruguay broke off diplomatic relations with Nazi Germany.
>
> This middle position was also that of Franco who, during the conflict of the Second World War, provided material and military support to the Germans in recognition of the help received during the Spanish Civil War. However, he did not enter the world conflict. Spain stationed armed forces in the Pyrenees to dissuade Germany from occupying it. In fact, the Franco regime, through its pragmatism, adopted a middle attitude in order to look after its interests.

Felix was an intellectual. He loved books, he read a lot. He was a loyal reader of the magazine *"Les Annales politiques et littéraires"* which published literary works, but also political, historical and artistic chronicles. The magazine was a great success, especially among the provincial bourgeoisie.

Felix was also a follower of Esperanto, a universal language born of the hope of a world unified by a single culture.

He, the diplomat who had had to defend his country's neutrality in the two world wars, when in 1914 his two brothers risked their lives and one of them had died for France, must have understood more than anyone else the need for peace.

Esperanto is an international language that is not the official language of any state. In 1887 Ludwik Zamenhof, under the pseudonym Doktoro Esperanto, published the project *"International Language"*. Esperanto is presented as an effective and economically equitable solution to the problem of communication between people of different mother tongues.

Esperanto was soon a great success. During these early years, Esperanto was essentially a written language. The first World Congress of Esperanto took place in 1905 in Boulogne-sur-Mer. It marked an important turning point for Esperanto. The language, which until then had been essentially written, was increasingly used for direct exchanges, especially at international meetings and congresses.

The First World War put a brake on the development of Esperanto, but it was revived in the 1920s by the enthusiasm generated by the hopes for peace that had emerged from the creation of the League of Nations. But the 1930s, with the rise of totalitarian regimes, and then the Second World War, marked a new halt to the development of Esperanto.

Today, Esperanto is an international language that, 130 years after its creation, is used by people from at least 120 countries around the world, including as a mother tongue.

Felix's fate had been a matter of chance, inadvertence, and error; Honoré, his father, did not know that in order for his son to be Uruguayan but also French like him, his birth had to be declared to the French authorities in Montevideo...

For the following children he did what was necessary, so they had a very different destiny from 1914 onwards...

13. 1914-1918 Emile and Jules Cestia

The period to which this chapter is devoted is marked by a major event: the war. But how can we talk about war, when we have not experienced it ourselves? A difficult exercise that I did not dare to tackle. I therefore preferred to let the witnesses speak through the letters that I transcribed.

In these letters we sometimes witness incredulously, sometimes with amazement, the parents' concern at the destructive patriotism of their 17-year-old son, and his rage to defeat the enemy, a warlike patriotism that little by little turns into a dream of glory.

The anguish of a grandmother who has "*cared for her grandchildren so much*" and who trembles every day with the fear of losing them, the misfortune of a young wife

who, after the happiness of her first child, sees her entire life turned upside down by her widowhood, are the sad realities of this war that are also revealed to us by these correspondences.

However, in the midst of the carnage of the soldiers on both sides, a light breeze of humanity and fraternity can be seen for a few hours when some soldiers, in order to bury their dead, disobey orders to kill each other.

So what can we say to those who claim that we have won the war of 1914? That their thinking must be qualified, because these testimonies show that in a war there may only be losers.

Emile Cestia

In 1910 Emile is summoned to the Board of Revision. The decision is *"classified as an auxiliary service"* because of a malformation in his left foot. He was therefore incorporated into the telegraph engineers where he served from 1910 to 1912

In May 1913, Emile was not yet 24 years old. He lived in Salon and was in the middle of preparing for a wedding to Fernande Gauthier who, like her sister-in-law Julie Laurens, was from Pélissanne.

Honoré, his father tells him that he will not be able to go to his wedding. He cites health problems that probably hide money problems linked to the economic crisis that was raging at the time. Indeed, his situation as a rentier exposed his resources to economic vicissitudes. This is what we learn from Felix's correspondence to his brother Emile.

Marseille, 26 May 1913

My dear brother,
It is with great sadness that I read in your letter that Papa was decidedly not coming to attend your wedding. I can easily understand your disappointment and the pain it must have caused you as well as your fiancée's parents. But having received a letter from papa the very day before yours, in which he said not a word, nothing, about your marriage, this silence surprised me very much and made me fear something. He only told me that my health left something to be desired; I had replied at once to urge them to come some time before and even to take advantage of it to go as far as Nice, but it became useless as a result of their decision which you announced to me afterwards. I wrote at the same time to let Jules come before and agree on the gift. I have not yet received an answer.

I see that you have received the papers, I hope in order [71]. As for the amount, and as agreed, I paid it, the translator having had the receipt presented the next day.

As was to be expected this Tuesday evening, you missed the train; consequently, these ladies have taken advantage of it to complete their purchases, so misfortune is always good for something!

No doubt you must be in the fever of preparations. Have you given orders for the furniture?

It seems to me that it would be better if you had them come as soon as possible, because this transport must be a hassle and you know you will have enough in the last days.

An idea occurs to me at this very moment, although perhaps it will not smile on you very much. Why don't you watch the ceremony again for a while and wait until Papa and Anna are well enough to be able to come? I submit it to you without hoping that it will seduce you.

I also wrote to grandmother to insist that she decide to come, arguing that her father is not so that she would represent the family alone

Did you receive a firm answer from Marie-Louise [72]

---

71 It is a letter dated 3 March 1913 in which Emile asked the consulate in Montevideo for an extract of his birth certificate and the death certificate of his mother Victorine Mothe. This letter is currently kept in the archives of Nantes.

72 Marie-Louise Sentubery married Lalanne, a first cousin of their mother Victorine Mothe. Marie-Louise lived in Tarbes.

Enclosed I send you these few verses [73] that I wrote about Pélissanne, which is also becoming your adopted homeland. I ask your indulgence for them, for they are in great need of it.

Our best memory to the Gauthier family, an affectionate hello to your future wife, and you, receive from us, two thousand (1000) kisses.

Titi Felipe (Your little Philippe)

On February 23, Fernande, Emile's wife, was about 7 weeks pregnant. The news quickly spread through the family. This is what we learn from Felix's correspondence with his brother and sister-in-law.

Marseilles, February 23, 1914

Dear Brother and Sister,

A deep and unexpected surprise caused us your letter announcing the novelty? And that your father and father-in-law confirmed to us during the visit made these days. A delay of only a few days was still necessary for the probabilities to become certainties. Have these been carried out? And, according to the cliché, the hopes of the dynasty seem to have received some realizations, which are employed in that obscure style of court news.

We hope that this does not upset you and that despite the trouble and hassle it causes, the news has seduced you.

With regret we see that you have given up on your trip!

If you want to accommodate yourself with our installation, you could come without any fear. Fernande and Lili would sleep in bed, Emile and I in a mattress on the floor. So you wouldn't have to go to a hotel. If you don't mind, just come along.

Maurice has long since cured of his cold, he is very well now. He is enjoying himself, he weighs 7k700 and already has two teeth. He likes to use jargon, he is wise and interesting.

Always heterophile, I see that you don't miss a single performance. Thus you went to see The Man Who Murdered [74] and Anna Karenina [75], precisely two plays taken from novels, and which are not worth them by much, even that of Farrère which, however, for my part is not unsympathetic to me. I much prefer Karenina, although the subject is violent and too pathetic.

We wish you a pleasant and joyful evening at the masked ball of the Cercle des Arts, where you intend to go, dressed in "tango and green empire" the comparison is

---

73 The worms have unfortunately been lost. Felix liked willingly, when an opportunity presented itself, to mark an event with a few verses.

74 *"The Man Who Murdered",* a play in four acts based on the novel by Claude Farrère published in 1913.

75 A stage adaptation of Tolstoy's novel.

typical, tango "last republican century" and green of the empire (history [anaine] and reactionary); you must have received, like us, news of Jules who is stunned by overwork. [76]

We are therefore waiting for you soon unless the separation from bed and board is too sad for you...

Our best remembrance to all yours and for you a thousand affectionate thoughts

Titi Felipe (ton petit Felipe)

Grandmother Madeleine, who was ill at the time of her son Emile's wedding, was finally decided to go to Salon, but unfortunately mobilization was decreed on August 1, 1914. Two days later, Germany declared war on France. His correspondence tells us of his emotion and his concern.

Louit on August 1, 1914

Mon Cher Emil,

I reply to your kind letter that you are in good health, and especially Fernande, who is well; poor friend; the sad news that prevents me from going to see you now that I have made up my mind; I was looking forward to seeing you, and especially little Maurice, who is so pretty and so pretty. Today I had a letter from Jules, it's not going well, poor friend, he's going to go to war, what a misfortune, and you, your father told me yesterday, maybe you too should leave, poor child. I am very unhappy. To my poor friends now we are reminded of the young men who have served and the mares who are good for the service [77]. I assure you, everyone is sad. I had taken care of myself so that I could go and see you, I was well, now think as I am going to be now. If you were to leave, write to me right away. Madame Hir gives you many compliments. You will give many compliments to the Gauthier family and you two receive a million kisses from your grandmother farewell Emile, Fernande

Madelaine Cestia

Jules is at war and we are worried about him but also about Emile, the young father who is also at risk of being mobilized. Felix writes to his brother.

Marseille, 24 September 1914

Dear Brother and Sister,

I see that nothing untoward has happened, and that the silence was only due to an oversight.

---

76 Jules then fulfilled his military obligations. Mobilization was decreed and war declared by Germany 6 months later in August 1914.

77 The French army, which was weakly motorized, needed horses.

Yesterday we received two words from Jules, where he told us that after having narrowly escaped and having fought for 6 consecutive days, he left the front to rest.

His company numbered only 91 men out of 250. As you can see, it's a real hecatomb. Finally, the main thing is that he is still safe and sound. Let it last until the end and it will be amazing. However, this threatens to last for a long time. You must have received a copy of the letters addressed to the house.

You must also have learned about the failure of Juan-Carlos' commitment, who is not old enough. Therefore it was wrong to want to present him as French, because then the birth certificate was essential, whereas in the Foreign Legion one is more fluid.

Marie-Louise asked me for information about the service in Tunis for Mrs. Pierre Bousquet who is to come and embark here. So I wrote to grandmother so that she could take the opportunity to be accompanied.

On your side, write to her so that she can make up her mind. Because I will tell you that she wrote to us and seems very depressed.

Perhaps it would be better for her to remain with us instead of alone, for she must be too bad-blooded.

The critical moment is approaching, no doubt with anxiety. I see that commemorating the present alliance you have chosen the names of the present sovereigns, but why [not] Jules for France instead of Raymond [78]. since its sovereign is called so, although he does not wear a Roman numeral. Moreover, why not Georgette since it is Georges that you choose if it is a boy. Apart from these minutiae, I find your idea very fortunate, and it will be one more memory of current events, although they will remain engraved until life.

As you say, Maurice has changed a lot, but he doesn't walk alone yet, only standing against the wall. He articulates a little but not distinctly what there is, he understands everything.

The consul has not yet returned, he must do so in October. It is therefore not possible to be absent at the present time [79].

From one moment to the next we were waiting for the announcement of Fernande's happy deliverance, to whom we wish good luck and great joy.

Will it be Georges or Alberte? Chi lo sa? [Who knows?] However, we will soon find out. With our best memories for all of yours, receive a million loving kisses from the three of us.

You Philip

---

78 Raymond Poincaré, President of the French Republic from 18 February 1913 to 18 February 1920.

79 Before becoming vice-consul of Uruguay, he acted as interim consul in the absence of the consul.

In her letters to her son Emile, grandmother Madeleine expresses her concern for Jules, her grandson, who is at the front and is delighted that Emile is still in Salon with his wife waiting for a happy event.

Louit, September 24, 1914

    Mon Cher Emil

    Yesterday I received your letter of the 21st, I see with pleasure that you are still in Avignon. As you tell me that you are close to the family and especially such a good family, I assure you that I appreciated them. You are very happy to have met so well. You had to deserve it, I'm very happy for you. I would have liked to see them again but it was impossible. They sent me a box of candy that I sent to Jules. He received them; he wrote to me the day before yesterday; he thanks me; he found them very good.

    He tells me that Mademoiselle Agnes has sent him a card from Rabastens; He was very happy to hear that I had this visit and I too only it was a bit short. I received a letter from Fernande with photos of the two sisters and her father and little Alberte. She is very beautiful and pretty, poor darling; I kiss him very often. I didn't give Fernande an answer. You will ask him for my apologies; As I don't write well, you'll thank these ladies for the box of candy they sent me.

    I think Jules will thank them. I told him that it was these ladies who had sent them to me; You will present my greetings to the whole family and you will receive a million kisses from your grandmother. To God; When you leave Avignon you will write to me. If you go to Tarbes and if you can't come, I'll go and see you in Tarbes. Jules sent me a photo of a baptism of a little baby; the godmother is seated on a cannon; There are 2 priests and officers. To God my friend

Madelaine Cestia

Louit on September 25, 1914

    Mon Cher Emil

    For so long that I have not given you any news of myself, I could not, I was trembling, impossible to live. Now, since I heard from Jules, I'm better. Yesterday I went to Tarbes, it had been 6 weeks since I had been there. Now I feel a little better. I am sending you yesterday's letter that Jules sent me. You'll see the poor guy if he had a narrow escape, [80] poor friend, I assure you, poor war. I believe that she will have life for me. We hear so many things, some say one thing, others say another, and all terrible things. In our country, young men or married, all left until the age of

---

80 See the account given with verve by Juan-Carlos in his letter of October 27, 1914, page 33.

42. [81] *If you saw the village how sad it is, and the markets, there is almost nothing. I was surprised yesterday, it had been so long since I had been there. Juquet Jean-Marie's dear [home] was wounded; it is near Toulouse. There are still so many deaths, that of dear Du malle is dead; Your father told me so yesterday.*

I received a letter from Fernande who told me that she was looking forward to being delivered; I'm also looking forward to good news; what a good thing you are not gone, poor friend, I received a visit from Madame Blond who spoke to me well of Jules. He helped her with the cooking; he always wanted to do something, poor friend. You will pay many compliments to the Gauthier family, and the two of you will receive from your grandmother my good heart, devoted to both of you. To God my friends

Madelaine Cestia

The good news has arrived in Tarbes. October 5, 1914 Marie-Louise Sentubery, married Lalanne, wrote to Emile Cestia

Tarbes 5 8bre1914 [82]

Dear Emile,
When it was time to close my letter, the postman handed me the mail. Among the correspondences I recognize the writing of a letter card and I say to my husband: this is probably the announcement of good news at Emile's. Eager to know its contents, I hasten to open it and my curiosity is satisfied. Therefore, dear Emile, without losing a minute, I hasten to address these lines to you, which I enclose with the letter that was ready to go, and I address to you and Fernande our sincere congratulations.

With what joy must you have received this precious offspring.

Your desires are fulfilled. A girl is a new bond that completes, that retempers, so to speak, your union. From now on you will live for someone other than yourself and unite all your hopes on a darling head.

I feel that my congratulations can add nothing at this moment to the happiness you must experience. But no one can prevent me from taking my part in all that may happen to you that is fortunate.

We wish you the continuation of your happiness and the prosperity of little Alberte (wishing you not to stop there) because she would be bored if you did not give her a little brother!

And then your happiness will be complete.

---

81 In fact, in August 1914, the mobilized classes ranged from 1896 (38 years and not 42) to 1913 (20 years).

82 8bre is an old abbreviation that designates the month of October and not the month of August.

You had a good idea to call her Alberte; it will be in memory of the tragic times we are living through.

The whole of France will keep the memory of King Albert for a long time, rather forever. [83]

Léon [Léon Lalanne her husband] and the whole family share in your joy and send you their good regards.

Marie-Louise

PS: best wishes for the speedy recovery of the young mother. In a few days, she will have forgotten the few hours of great pain, to think only of her happiness!

In the last months of 1914, Honoré and Madeleine exchanged many letters with their son and grandson Emile. The grandmother's letters are full of her emotions, while Honoré remains more modest in his.

Thursday, October 15, 1914

Dear sons,

My mother has asked me to reply to your letters of 17 and 28 September and 3 October. She tells me to excuse her if she doesn't write to you, her hand trembles a little and her vision is also blurred when she stares a little. She recommends that you do not get tired of writing. After a few days she was not very well but now she is better. She suffers a lot from the cold of her feet, which causes her headaches. Because of everything that is happening, as there are so many dead and wounded – here and in the surrounding area in Aureilhan we have 10 dead and in Louit out of 4 who have gone to the fire 3 injured, the one from Tampano has come back for 15 days, the one from Piquet also – she likes to hear them and it hurts her. She fears for Jules, let's hope he will come back to us. She told me to tell you that she regretted not having been able to go and see you, but she was not too well and could not leave the cattle as they had no one with her. But she was very happy when she heard of Juliette's arrival that your sister had been lifted and above all that everything had gone well. Many kind things to the Gauthier family and while waiting for the pleasure of reading you, they kiss all 3 of you.

H Cestia

PS: As for Jules, I received 2 words last night in which he sent me back [...] the money order I had sent him on August 13, telling me that we had not wanted to pay him because part D was missing, you must know what it is, the fault of some employee. I was reimbursed for it. He told me to send him bank [notes] in a letter instead. It's very annoying for him. He doesn't tell me yet that he has received the 3 packages I sent him, he told me that he has received yours, let's hope he will receive

---

83 Albert 1st of Belgium decided in August 1914 to resist Germany.

them. Last Monday, I sent him a waterproof canvas that he had asked me for for the rain, 120 wide by 150, I put a can of sardines in it, a little sugar. I saw on the newspapers that it is forbidden to send food provisions, but I hope it will reach him anyway. We embrace you all.

H Cestia

Louit, November 2

Mon Cher Emil

Yesterday I received a letter from Jules who tells me that he has received 5 parcels that you and Felix and your father sent him and Mr. Candebat and Blon he was sent a sausage, and he told me that it must be from Soreac [84]. Victorine must have carried it from her mother; he was very good; the same day he was appointed sergeant, he told me that a bottle of Monfoconton wine would have been needed.

I also sent him two pairs of stockings that I made for him and then I gave your father 5 francs to buy him provisions; now he will have received everything. Your father told me on Thursday that you too had to go; In your last letter you don't tell me. To poor friend, I am very unhappy to see that two months ago I was so happy to have a great little lady who is the only one in the family; your father [had] boys, Felix a boy; Take good care of her, the poor little darling. In the hope of seeing her if this sad war should cease and poor Jules should return, and even before I die I will go and see her, and little Maurice you will kiss him for me, my little one, and you will write to me at once if you have to leave. To my poor friends, I who have cared for you so much, I did not believe in treating you for such a war, that if I did not give you an answer each time, write to me. You are married, my poor friends. You'll do well to compliment the Gauthier family and the rest of you two receive the best caresses from your grandmother. To God, my good friends, and without forgetting little Alberte, my little one,

Madelaine Cestia

Louit, November 19

Mon Cher Emil,

I received your letter the day before yesterday with one from Jules who told me that you sent him a package and that he received it very well, thank you for him. I was very glad of it, poor Jules; if we could nurse him enough to make him come back; afterwards [without him] I would be bored with the rest of you. I have made him two pairs of socks which I will give to your father to send him with other provisions. When I sent the others I gave your father 5 francs to put him provisions,

---

84 Castéra-Lou, where the Sentubery and Soreac families come from, are villages that adjoin Louit to the north.

but I will make him stockings as long as he stays there. You tell me that I do not tremble; There are times in the morning, when I get up, then I don't tremble; Then there are times. Jules tells me that he has experienced that my hand trembles and that my eyesight changes, and it's true, but when I write to Jules, I feel an emotion, my heart sinks. They came back 3 wounded, the one from Cher [at] Priquet and Dalier and the one from Cher [at] Camparo, he saw himself with Jules. I assure you that he told me it's terrible and they all left.

You tell me that you have a visit from Felix and the family and Juan-Carlos. I did not see him; Your father told me so, but he is not [...]. You tell me that little Maurice looks like his father, it's true. In the photograph, your father told me that he looked like his father and so did I; and little Alberte, who does she look like, the papa or the mamma, the little cutie whom I love very much. If I were a swallow I would go and see her. But see you later, take care of her well. You will pay many compliments to the Gauthier family and you receive a million kisses from your grandmother and not forgetting Fernande and little Alberte to God my friends

Madelaine Cestia

Aureilhan, December 10, 1914

Dear sons,

I am replying to your letter of 16 9 September85 [] in which we see with pleasure that you are all in good health and that little Alberte is increasing every day by about 30 gr hope that this will continue As for us, still more or less, except for Anna who has been ill, she is a little better. André [7 years old] also had a cold.

You tell us that you had a visit from Juan-Carlos and that it is hilarious, that it has amused you a lot. I think he must be bored, I often see him always alone on foot or on a bicycle.

As for Jules I received news from him yesterday, he is still well He tells us that he spent 4 days of rest very well that they had fun, they found [?] and good. He told us that he had received your package on the 29th. We send him some every week, he receives a little from all sides and as things are going so badly and the postal parcels are slow to arrive, we will suspend the gifts of the 1st of the year for this year and we will send one more parcel to Jules.

As you tell me that now you can get some securities in the banks, I can't touch any of them yet, except for a few from the State, I have to get money loaned, let's hope it won't last too long.

Here there is nothing new to tell you except that Madame Sempe wanted to commit suicide; She shaved a razor in the throat but she didn't die.

---

85 9bre is an old abbreviation that designates the month of November and not that of September.

Many kind things from Anna and André to all of you as well as the Castane Houley families and Poineau
Your father kissing the three of you

H Cestia

PS Our Friendships to the Gauthier Family

On December 10, 1914, Madelaine wrote to her grandson Emile.

Louit, December 10

Mon Cher Emil

I am replying to your kind letter of November 26. I am pleased to see that you are all well. As for me, for the moment, I'm pretty good. Today I received a card from Jules. He tells me that he is good, if he tells me the truth. Here it is now said that they are going to make a great struggle, this faith he will not escape. Now I am going to spend a few very bad days.

I made him 6 pairs of socks and your father sent them to him and I started them [yours] I'm going to send you a package before Christmas. Your father will send them to me, and I'll do the same for Jules. Anna is sick, on Thursday your father told me so. He never talks to me about her and on Thursday he told me that the doctor had found her very thin, that she was anaemic. He her twice a day with morphine and Mrs. Molezen told me that she was a real escablete and that she thought she was going away from the chest. And so your father is not happy and he doesn't get a penny of interest. Vila has given him some and he borrows; he told me so on Thursday, and that he would be embarrassed to take care of her. Here there are about twenty men now, only the old people remain, it's sad; there are houses without men; It is said that it will last for another 2 years. That's not possible. You will present my greetings to the Gauthier family and you two will receive a million kisses from your grandmother and not forgetting little Alberte whom you will kiss for me. I compliment you; You told me she looked like her daddy.

To God my friends

Madelaine Cestia

Emile finally left the Salon post office in September 1915. Sapper Emile Cestia of the Eighth Engineer Regiment died for France as a result of his wounds at the volunteer hospital of Berck Plage on September 21, 1918.

His wife Fernande was helped a lot by her sister Agnès, who was unmarried. After Fernande's death in 1952, Agnès Gauthier, a long-time municipal councillor in Pélissanne, was a precious help to her niece.

Jules Cestius

In 1914, the internet did not exist. Grandmother Madeleine wrote frequently to Felix, Emile and Jules. Only the letters addressed to Emile have reached me; the other correspondence has probably been lost.

Jules was mobilized at the beginning of the war of 1914. When he was younger, and without family responsibilities, he was exposed to more risks than his brother Emile. Luck for him, bad luck for Emile, Jules will return from the war.

> Jules Cestia Campaign against Germany
>
> Quote: An intelligence officer of great cold blood. During a period of two battles, he was able to collect and transmit the most valuable information on enemy movements and organizations in a very difficult situation. Ensured the supply of ammunition to the 1st line despite heavy enemy machine-gun fire.
>
> Under the intelligence officer of admirable courage and enthusiasm during the fighting. Directed his observation service with calm and method, going himself to the most exposed places to locate machine gunners who were hindering our progress. Thus collected commands valuable for the command. Croix de Guerre was entitled to wear the fourragère of the 57th Infantry Regiment.

On January 8, 1915, for the New Year, Jules wrote a letter to Agnès Gauthier, his sister-in-law's sister. We find in this letter a testimony of a little fraternity between French and German soldiers that I thought it would be interesting to transcribe here.

Beaulne [86], 8 January 1915

Dear Agnes,
I hasten to thank you for the good wishes and wishes that you have kindly expressed in your kind letter of December 22.
In my turn, I wish you and your family happiness and prosperity for the year that is beginning.
May 1915 mark the fall of the German Empire, the revenge for the injury done to Alsace and Lorraine, and give us a favorable peace leading to the beginning of an era of prosperity, of a resumption of affairs.
Unfortunately, we are not yet at that fine day, and many brave men will fall, blood will be shed before the end of hostilities!!
I am currently in the 2nd line very quiet for the moment, annoyed only by the rain that comes through the roof of the hut.
During the day, it was forbidden to go out on pain of receiving shells; During the night for 2 days I have been sleeping like a groundhog.

---

86 The current name is Vendresse-Beaulne. The commune was created in 1923 by the merger of the communes of Beaulne-et-Chivy and Vendresse-et-Troyon.

I don't think I told Emile what happened to us on December 29th.

That day we were in a trench 50 meters from the Boches. From 8 a.m. they shouted "Comrades, come closer, we won't shoot" But no one moved, knowing too well their bad faith. A German throws cigarettes and biscuits at us. Seeing that no one is disturbed, he quietly goes to look for them. A sergeant of the 1st Cnie of the 57th then came out of the trench, a Boche captain did the same and came to shake hands with our NCO.

He talked with the latter and suggested that he let 6 Frenchmen killed near their trench be buried. It is accepted.

The Germans and the French dug a pit together at an equal distance from the 2 trenches. The burial over, we greet each other and everyone goes home.

On January 1st, these same Boches apparently drank champagne with ours. I don't want to say for sure because I didn't see him having been relieved on the 29th at 7 p.m.

Do you know what the Minister of War has offered us as gifts?

2 apples, 3 nuts, dates, a bottle of champagne at 5. As a sergeant I had my half-bottle. The day before we had half a liter of wine.

These are certainly some sweets, but they do not diminish the regret we feel at being far from our loved ones and those we love.

Looking forward to reading you or better to seeing you again, receive, dear friend and your family, the expression of my cordially devoted sentiments.

J Cestia

On his return from the war, Sergeant Jules Cestia settled for a while in Marseille, then in Toulouse in 1922 and in Louit, his native village, which he left in November 1925 to marry in Aureilhan. He then gave up his job as a postal employee and devoted himself, with his wife Thérèse, to the farm in Aureilhan.

14.   1914-1918 Juan-Carlos Dupont

Juan-Carlos, the youngest son of Dominique Dupont, Honoré Cestia's partner in the shoe trade, was just over 16 years old in 1914. While a student in a military school in Montevideo, to the great desolation of his parents, he came to France, his *"Second homeland"* in his own words, to enlist and fight against the Germans. He will show extraordinary enthusiasm and determination in this project. The letters he sent to his parents are a direct, spontaneous, authentic, and straightforward testimony to this period of our history.

During his stay in France, Juan-Carlos met his family from France, the Cestia family – Dominique Dupont and Honoré Cestia, had forged close ties in Montevideo – but also with the Lallanne family, his father's first cousins with whom he stayed. This period was thus an opportunity for the parents in Montevideo and their son Juan-Carlos in Tarbes, as well as for Marie-Louise Lalanne also in Tarbes, to exchange an abundant correspondence, of which I give here a few excerpts. [87]

Letter from Dominique Dupont 5/8/1914

Montevideo, August 5, 1914

My very dear Cousin [88],
The purpose of this letter is to announce to you news that will surprise you. There is my son Juan-Carlos who is leaving for France, to present himself as a volunteer in the French army.

On the Lutetia, 1,500 young people embarked in Buenos Aires and 400 French and foreign people in Montevideo. Juan-Carlos is part of this expedition that will land in Bordeaux or Marseille. As the agency did not know which of the two ports this boat would go to, I quickly wrote to Felix Cestia to tell him about this news. If J. Carlos goes to Marseilles, if he can, he will go and pay him a visit, at the same time to ask him to guide him if he needs it.

Seeing J. Carlos' decision, we were all left without knowing what was happening to us. There was no way to change his mind, he leaves very happy.
(...)
The effects of the European war began to make its effects felt in commerce and industry. Everything, even the most indispensable for life, costs much more. Now the government has just decreed to close the stock exchange and all the banks for

---

87 Out of a total of 8 letters from Dominique to his cousin Marie-Louise and 52 letters from Juan-Carlos translated from Spanish by his son Lionel Dupont.

88 Marie-Louise Sentubery married Léon Lalanne, daughter of Jean Sentubery was born in France, lived in Montevideo until her marriage in Oleac-Débat.

10 days, and for three months no one will have the right to convert the banks' issue for gold. This causes great harm.

(...)

Dear cousin, our thoughts are still on what may happen to J. Carlos, my heart sinks, I can no longer write.

(...)

While waiting for your good news, Farewell my dear cousin. Please accept the assurance of our tender affections.

Domingo Dupont [89]

Letter from Dominique Dupont 1/9/1914

Montevideo, 1er Septembre 1914

My dearest Cousin,

(...)

The Lutetia left Montevideo on August 24th. As he expects to make the crossing to Bordeaux in 11 days, at the time you receive this letter, I believe you will have had the pleasure of seeing J. Carlos. So as soon as you receive this one, have the goodness to answer me at once and tell me all you know about J. Carlos. We look forward to hearing from him.

Dear cousin, this time I am sending you only the statement of your current account, which was closed at the end of August with a balance in your favour of 230.54 piastres for the rent of your house for the months of June and July.

I was kind enough to send you, as usual, a cheque for the said sum, but I could not find any bank that would guarantee the receipt of this sum. It appears, from what I was told in a bank, that if I were to send you a cheque, it would not be paid at this moment in France either.

Before the European war, there was a great crisis in Montevideo, as in all the countries of the world. The war has increased it. Many workers are out of work, and trade is completely paralyzed.

Before, in the main streets, there were no houses to rent to set up a business. Today, empty houses for rent can be found everywhere, at lower prices. Your tenants start asking for discounts. Those who complained were Messrs. Bacherelli and Rossi. If these tenants remain firm to their claims, before they see the empty houses, I will give them a small discount.

(...)

Domingo Dupont

Letter from Juan-Carlos Dupont 10/9/1914

---

89 Dominique Dupont, Dominique in the civil registry was born in France. In 1914, he was 52 years old. He left France 40 years ago. He then signed "Domingo".

Aboard the Lutetia, September 10, 1914

My dearest Mother,

As I promised you, I will write to you from the first port where I arrive. For the moment I don't know if it will be Dakar or San Vicente. We are indeed 6 hours from the finish and we have not been told anything yet.

The day after we left, at 3 a.m., we met a German warship waiting for us. But as soon as he saw it, the commander made his way south, by forced march, and we were able to escape. So far, the trip has been splendid: I eat well, I sleep "macanudo" [90] and I keep a lot of enthusiasm as well as my companions. As soon as I arrive in Bordeaux I will write to you.

And is Dad better? And you, are you well? Don't let him eat "Chorizos" and sausage.... Keep them for me!

The man with the beard is scolding me for writing in pencil. In "8 days" we will be in "Paris de francia". Tell "Tio Luis" that I will bring him 8 hairs of the Kaiser's beard, because the others I have already promised. I can't write to you better, the boat moves a lot. About 80 percent of passengers became seasick. I was lucky enough to escape it.

(...)

Best memories to "Tio and Tia Luis", a kiss to Grandma Anita, Mama-señora, Bon-papa, to the "Potota" and to you and Daddy (may he keep the sausages for me) "a fuerte abrazo" from your "son"

Juan-Carlos Cacalo

Remembrance to all who will ask for me
Long live my mom and dad!
Hip, Hip, Hip Hurrah !

Letter from Juan-Carlos Dupont 22/9/1914

Tarbes, Tuesday, September 22, 1914
to Mrs. Eugenie M. Dupont
I'm in my mother,

This is the fourth letter that I have written to you, and I am very surprised that I have not yet received an answer.

Our trip from Montevideo to Bordeaux was splendid. We were 2,400 passengers. The governor of the island told91 us that we had escaped by the greatest of chances. Indeed, we were chased by German warships all the way. The food they gave us was worse than the food we give to dogs, and there was little of it.

---

90 The best translation would be "Au poil" (according to Lionel Dupont).

91 It must be the island of Cape Verde.

When I arrived in Bordeaux, I received a letter from Marie-Louise telling me to come. I took the train at 9:30 a.m., after having supped with Ducousseau, Peyrou, the two Laborde brothers, Durand and all those who signed the postcard I sent you.

We arrived in Tarbes the next day, at three o'clock in the afternoon, after a painful journey. We were very well received.

As they told you, in the letter that Aunt sent you, it is impossible for me to commit myself despite all the desire I have to do so. I'm waiting for your instructions, I don't know what I'm going to do.

(...)

With nothing more for the moment, your son leaves you and Papa, sending you a very strong kiss for Mama-Señora and Bon-papa

Juan-Carlos

Letter from Juan-Carlos Dupont 22/10/1914

Marseilles, October 22, 1914

Dear little daddy,

(...)

The city of Tarbes is quite large and pretty. Wide bike lanes are everywhere, but what I like most is the cleanliness, order and tranquility that reigns there.

(...)

My cousin Emile who got married more than a year ago and had a little girl 17 days ago. I received a letter from Felix in which he told me to go and pay him a visit. I asked M. Louise's opinion and made up my mind.

(...)

Marseille is a very lively city. Every day French colonies of English, Hindu, Senegalese, Japanese, Canadian and Arab troops arrived. The Germans were terribly afraid of these men because, when they took prisoners, they cut off their heads and cut off their ears to make necklaces around their bodies. I have seen a lot of them.

(...)

Juan-Carlos

Tell Angelita that she'll iron my suit and ties. He doesn't have the fold. Right away!

In a few days I will send you some journals of this war. Best memories of Felix and Peyrou. The latter is going to war in four days. The three Labordes as well.

Chàu [92]

---

92 It is a colloquial and slang expression specific to the Rio de la Plata and used to say goodbye to a friend. A form of greeting and a term of friendship that is mainly masculine. At the same time, it means "goodbye and see you soon". You would certainly have recognized it if I had

Letter from Juan-Carlos Dupont 27/10/1914

Marseilles, October 27, 1914

Dear Mom,

    As I told you in my last letter, I made it my duty to go to Marseilles to visit my cousin Felix.

    When I arrived, I was very well received by my cousin "Lili", who is very good and friendly, as well as by my little cousin "Mimi" who is very cute, beautiful and tall, but who does not yet walk because he has a weakness in his legs.

    They had intended to make a trip to America, but this cursed war prevented them from doing so.

    My other cousin, Jules, as you know, is at the front where he almost died four times. The first time, it was a piece of shrapnel that went through his ear, slightly injuring him. The second time, it was a shell that passed under his arm, tearing the hood to shreds without hitting the flesh. The next time he was appointed corporal.

    The last one, the one in which he came closest to death, went like this: The sergeant had to do an errand. And as he was there, he told him to remain on guard to watch the provisions. Suddenly, the order to attack was given to the company, but he could do nothing but stay there to keep the supplies until the sergeant returned. Luckily, the sergeant did not return until 2 o'clock. Of the company that initially consisted of 90 men, only 8 men remained. He says that if it had not been for the food, he would also have stayed there with his comrades. He says that in this way he escaped from certain death. The war was very bloody. Men drop like flies. I have 15 acquaintances of the "Lutetia" who died. The end result, you may be sure, is that we shall defeat those dirty and filthy Germans. Every day I see them. France is full of them. In Tarbes alone, there are more than 3,000 of them.

    As for me, in spite of my efforts, it has not yet been possible for me to enlist. But I still have one way, and that is to wait until February to turn 17 and introduce myself.

    (...)

    My other cousin Emile had a little girl 15 days ago. He lives in Salon, 60 kilometres from Marseille. I have just received a letter in which Emile invites me to spend 2 days at his place. But it doesn't seem possible to me, because I've already written to Marie-Louise to tell her that I'm going away on Saturday.

---

transposed it into the French derivative form of "tchao". It is of the same nature as the "Che" (Tché, as in the nickname given to "Che Guevara" to mark his Argentine origins). The two locutions are often combined in the "Chaù chè" to further increase the friendly and familiar character of the greeting. The "ché" is indeed a form of "tu" only used in Argentina and Uruguay and ignored by the Spanish and other South American countries... (note by Lionel Dupont).

We visited the city with Felix. It is very beautiful, but has the defect of being very dirty. I will send you many views. There is Notre Dame which is 300 meters high, from where you can contemplate the panorama of the whole city, the surroundings, the countryside, and all the forts that are at sea.

(...)
Memories to all as well as to the "Oriental" Uruguayans
Phew! Phew! Phew!

Letter from Dominique Dupont 24/10/1914

Montevideo, le 24 Octobre 1914

Dear cousin,
(...)
On the 2nd of this month, I also received a letter from Jules Cestia which he sent me from Libourne on July 31, a few days before leaving for the war. This letter arrived after 2 months and 3 days. I have heard from you and from Felix that he has been wounded, and I hope that this wound will not have serious consequences.

Dear cousin, you cannot imagine the effect that your last letter has had on us, when you learn of the steps you have taken, as soon as you heard that J. Carlos was going to arrive in France, on board the Lutetia to enlist as a volunteer for the war. You would have liked to go and join him when he landed, when without waiting for him you received his visit at Tarbes, on the 13th of last month.

We were very happy when we learned that neither at the time of Bordeaux's nor at Tarbes' recruitment, they wanted to enlist him for age. This news gave us and his ancestors a great deal of pleasure. They cried with joy when they saw that they did not want to allow him to possibly go and be massacred. It appears, from the news, that it is a most terrible war.

(...)

Domingo Dupont

Letter from Juan-Carlos Dupont 10/11/1914

Tarbes, November 10, 1914

Dear Mom,
(...)
After visiting Marseille very well, we went to spend 3 days in Salon, where I was introduced to his wife Fernande, who is very cold. Emile's wife has a sister who is a teacher. She plays the piano and sings very well. I myself sang and danced a tango that he liked very much. She asked me to get her some Tangos and that she would pay for them. But I told her that my sister had old and very pretty ones. So I ask you, please, to send me some of them, for example 8 to 10.

(...)

Juan-Carlos

Many kisses to my 3 grandparents and to the Potota.

Memories to Angelita and to all those who ask after for me.

Letter from Dominique Dupont 12/11/1914

Montevideo, November 12, 1914

My dearest cousin,

(...)

I am happy to learn that your brother is in Lourdes, in the nurses' section and that Emile Cestia has been mobilized in the post office in Salon. Which will be exempted from the events of the war, it was not the same with Jules Cestia and my nephew Jean-Marie, although they are only wounded, they paid with their blood for the fruit of this tragic period.

We think that you have acted very well, having agreed with Mr. Gardey Firmin that he should not give J. Carlos a false statement. Although he regrets not going to war, perhaps some day he will understand how fortunate he was not to have exposed himself to the rigors of this war. You will present my best regards to Mr. Gardey Firmin, whom I immediately remembered, and you will pay him many compliments.

Dear cousin, enclosed you will find the statement of your current account closed at the end of October, with a balance in your favor of $699.18, the amount of the rent for your house for the months of August and September. As soon as there are no inconveniences, I will send you the said sum.

You know that to the tenant, Mr. Bacherelli, at the end of October, I gave him a discount of five dollars a month. The other tenants, for the moment, pay the same price, having told them that I had no order from you to lower the rents. At the house of the tenant Bacherelli, I was obliged to make some small repairs, the mason has not yet given me his account.

(...)

Domingo Dupont

Letter from Juan-Carlos Dupont 11/1/1915

Tarbes, January 11, 1915

My dearest little mother,

(...)

I very much regret that many of my letters have been lost, because of a wrong address. I don't know if you received, about twenty days ago, a photo where I was a French soldier. In case you have not received it, keep the one I am sending you with this letter. If you have received it, give it to my dearest Bon-papa and Mamaseñora. The piece of cloth I am sending you, you must keep it as a souvenir of the war. It was taken on a German war aeroplane by a friend who is a soldier and who gave it to me as a gift. I also have five bullets, different uniform buttons that I think I'll give to Dad when I come back to my beloved country again. I make six major collections

on the war which are published in magazines. I am not sending them to you because you would have to pay a lot of fees at the post, but I renew that I will bring them back to you when I come back.
(...)

Letter from Dominique Dupont 16/1/1915

Montevideo, January 16, 1915

My dearest cousin
(...)
From the news you give me, it seems that this accursed war is one of the most barbarous, and to think that there are people who say that among the Teutons there is civilization. These in Montevideo are the least. The greater part of the world gives them the name of savages. In the Montevideo press you will not find a newspaper that defends the Germans. It is recognized by all: the Germans have no other inclination than to make people suffer. For all these things, we are very happy to know that J. Carlos, with you, is beyond the reach of these barbarians. However, he believes he will succeed in incorporating by the time he is 17 years old. As I am not of his opinion, I will not send him the consent he has asked of me. What remorse would it be for us if he fell wounded, if he lost an arm, a leg, in short, if he remained mutilated for the rest of his life... In view of the news that you often receive from various cousins and friends who are at the front letting you know the fatigues, miseries and dangers to which they are exposed at every moment, I cannot understand how all this news does not change J. Carlos' mind.
(...)
Dear cousin, as I have no further inconvenience in sending you the amount of the rent for your house, you will find enclosed a cheque for the sum of (5,158 Frs,50) five thousand one hundred and fifty-eight francs and fifty centimes, equivalent to the exchange of 5.43 ($950 - nine hundred and fifty piastres) for the rents of the months of June, July, August, September, October and November 1914, as well as the statement from your current account at the end of December 1914 with a balance of ($921.06 Nine hundred and twenty-one piastres and six centimes), the amount of the rents on your house up to the end of November 1914. This time, I was able to get a very advantageous exchange. The bank of Montevideo has informed me that this cheque can be presented at the branch of the Crédit Lyonnais in Tarbes.
(...)

Domingo Dupont

Letter from Juan-Carlos Dupont 7/2/1915

Tarbes, February 7, 1915

Chers parents

(...)
Every day, I feel more and more enthusiastic about this piece of France which is my second home. Everyone tells me that it's time to get involved. It is certain that I will not go to the battlefield because it takes at least 2 or 3 months of training and young men of about my age, they will only send them at the last moment, when the peace has been signed, to keep the cities we have occupied in Germany. So you can sleep, and be very quiet about me, for it will only be a fine walk to Berlin. What do you think? Isn't that a good idea?
(...)
In the authorization you are to send me, you must state that I am the son of a Frenchman, that I am 17 years old and that I am enlisting only for the duration of the war. It must also be signed by the Consul of France.
(...)
Peyrou asks me that you do not tell Montevideo that he was in the trenches. Say, on the contrary, that he is in a hospital as a nurse. This way, his mother will have less bad blood.

Juan-Carlos Dupont

Letter from Dominique Dupont 21/3/1915

Montevideo, le 21 Mars 1915

My dearest cousin
(...)
Dear cousin, concerning J. Carlos' expenses, as it was not we who advised him to go to war, he must not think that he can abuse our kindness towards his useless expenses. You will tell him on my behalf that he must do his best to spend the least. We are not in a position to spend much. The money we gave him when he left should have been enough for him for a lot longer. After he has exhausted his small capital, you tell us that you give him 5 francs a week and that some weeks this quantity is not enough for him. At his request, you have satisfied his desire. Since he has nothing to think about, that you buy him what he needs, we find that this is a lot what you give him, to a child like him, without experience or reflection... The more money he is given, the more he spends. It would be a disservice to do him a disservice, and it would be an inducement to create vices. He must therefore make do with less than 5 francs per week. Try to give him less.
The only thing I wouldn't look at would be the fees that would have to be incurred if he wanted to study.
(...)

Domingo Dupont

Letter from Dominique Dupont 21/5/1915

Montevideo, may 21, 1915

My dearest cousin,
(...)
Since J. Carlos is always of the same opinion - he persists in wanting to follow his stubbornness to go to war, I have always recognized him in all his letters: it seems that he was born to be a soldier - I don't know whether I did right or wrong, in agreement with Eugenie, I sent him my consent. He must have received it.
(...)

Domingo Dupont

Letter from Juan-Carlos Dupont 9/5/1915

Tarbes, 9 May 1915

Chers parents
After so many months of doing nothing, without working and spending so much money, I can finally give you great news that will cause you a lot of joy, because I believe that now my career is assured.
You thought I would never become a man. Well, here is the contrary proof! Thanks to your consent, I was able to join the 14th Artillery Regiment. But I will never go to the fire, otherwise quite the opposite. When I introduced myself to the Colonel, I was immediately sympathetic to him, especially when I told him that I had been to the military school in Montevideo. So he said to me, "I'm going to make you a man." Immediately he spoke to the captain to ask him to put me in the platoon to move to the rank of "Brigadier". I believe that by studying as I study, in less than 4 months I will have the rank and then they will put me in the training of young recruits. Doesn't that sound like a good idea to you? You can ask Tía how happy I am.
(...)

I will write you a letter every week telling you about everything that happens to me in military life. You're happy, aren't you! Many memories to the Potota, to my dear grandparents, to Uncle and Aunt, to the Beba, to Angelita and to everyone in general and you receive a million kisses and kisses from

Charles.

Many memories of uncle and aunt and all those here.
My address: Charles Dupont: 14th Artillery Regiment, 65th Battery- 2nd Gun Tarbes (HP) Now my name is no longer Juan-Carlos, but Charles.

Letter from Juan-Carlos Dupont 20/5/1915

Tarbes, May 20, 1915

Dear Mom,
(...)
Here I meet many Americans who come in the same conditions as mine. I have very good friends and am very reasonable. When I come back to Montevideo you will

no longer recognize your Juan-Carlos, so shy and fearful and ill-mannered, in short you will find nothing wrong with me because now I know what life is and am no longer a kid but a man.

(...)

Charles.

Many memories of the whole Lalanne family.
Adios

Letter from Juan-Carlos Dupont 20/6/1915

Tarbes, 20 June 1915

Dear "Mamita" and Dad

I'm writing to tell you that I'm in the best health in the world, as I am sure you all are at home.

I will now tell you about my life as a soldier. I never imagined that military life in France would be so joyful and fun. Everyone loves me because I make myself loved by being a good companion and having a cheerful character. All the officers esteem me very much, and whatever I ask for, they grant me. I am a very good soldier, but what makes me stand out from the others is that I am very agile on horseback and I have a lot of courage for the jumps at the bar which is 1m20 high and as I have a good horse I jump them very well without stirrups and by letting go of the reindeer. I tell you this because the Captain who gives lessons congratulated me.

This week, we had exams and I can tell you that I got very good grades, but I must add that they take into account my arrival from America and my inexperience with the French language.

Here, I find myself with a lot of Americans and we often talk about this beautiful country that is America. On the other hand, I can't see these people from the Hautes-Pyrénées and especially the Basques who are uneducated and rough-hewn people. To speak frankly, I will tell you that America is a thousand times better than France.

Yesterday we went to the "Shooting Range". You would have seen what the explosions were doing. It is a terrible thing that the quantity of earth they caused to rise.

The most important thing I have to tell you is the arrival of the President of the French Republic to visit the arsenal of Tarbes. And as we had to pay him the honors, I had the honor of seeing him pass 2 meters from me.... You can imagine how happy I was!

In my next letter, I will send you the photographs, taken by a friend of mine who is also a soldier, son of Colonel Parias. On one of them, I mounted my horse, the revolver in my belt and the sword at my side. On the other, I am next to a 75 mm gun.

Give lots of kisses to Mamaseñora, Bonpapa, Potota, and the two of you, receive a million kisses from a future officer of the French army.

Juan-Carlos
Many memories of the Lalanne family
PS: This letter is written in pencil and badly written, because I now have to go out on horseback.
Letter from Juan-Carlos Dupont 21/8/1915

Tarbes, August 21, 1915

Dear mom and dad,
(...)
Now, I'm going to tell you two or three episodes of my military life. Nearly a month ago a factory which works for the army, and whose employees are almost all Spaniards, and therefore Germanophiles, went on strike. They began to howl against France, and then a platoon of 40 men, or rather young men, were sent from the nearest barracks, which was ours, because they are all my age. We went there with bayonets and made many arrests, and as I knew Spanish, they put me as interpreter. But thanks to the arrangements made by our captain, things passed without unpleasant incident.
(...)

Juan-Carlos

I will write you a long letter every 15 days and a postcard twice a week. Will you do the same for me?
Adios, Adios, Chàu, Chàu
Letter from Juan-Carlos Dupont 17/11/1915

Tarbes, November 17, 1915

Dear Mom,
(...)
From the first days of my arrival in France, I shared with Marinette (my little cousin) a great sympathy and friendship. This friendship grew day by day, until the hour arrived when I confessed to him that I loved him. After several interviews, she told me that she was still too young to think about love [she was 15 years old] but she gave me her consent to continue to see us in secret from everyone. Thus passed my first four months. We talked to each other when we were alone. I often went to pick her up after school.

Day by day our relations became closer, but unfortunately the day came when we were discovered for the first time. This happened in the following way because Aunt had realized that I had taken the affection she has for her brother and perhaps also for her parents. One day (February 2nd) I was invited to a wedding, with the whole family. We set out first with Marinette, Jean my uncle, and aunt had stayed because she was not yet ready, but above all to look in my pocket-book, which I had forgotten in a room, and in which I had been imprudent enough to leave four love-letters from Marinette. This is how we were discovered. Aunt scolded Marinette very loudly, but she told me how it had all happened, so that I could be on my guard when Aunt came to tell me about it. This happened two days later, when Aunt came to say to me, "What intentions do you have towards Marinette?" Then I replied, as we had agreed with Marinette, "I have no other intention than to love her as my own sister." Since that day we have never spoken to each other about it again. But the romantic relationships continued stronger than ever, undermining her parents' surveillance.

When the day of my departure to the regiment arrived, Marinette did everything she could to prevent me from leaving. She became angry, and we remained nearly a month without speaking to each other or writing to each other. Finally she wrote to me again and we made peace. After this there was another little quarrel which lasted a week, because Marinette, jealous like all women, took my pocket-book and searched it, and one day it chanced that she found letters sent me by a young lady named Rita, who ran after me a great deal, and to whom I paid no attention. These incidents helped to strengthen his love for me more closely.

One day, when I was returning from Bordeaux, I went to my Aunt's house and greeted her as I was used to, I found it strange that she answered me with great coldness. When I asked her the reason for this, she had me read a letter which she was going to send to me at the regiment, in which she said that she had discovered our love, reproaching me for them rather harshly, and as she feared that we would continue our relations, she told me not to come to her house for a while, in order to leave, to Marinette and myself, the time to forget each other. But Aunt is completely mistaken, because it is just the opposite. I receive letters almost every day and I reply to him through someone who is very interested in us.

I had intended to send you all the letters that Marinette sent me, but as there are nearly 50 of them, I will take them to you myself in America.

(...)

Juan-Carlos

This letter is badly written because of the night. The electric light has gone out, as is the candle that illuminates me.

Letter from Juan-Carlos Dupont 28/11/1915

Tarbes, November 28, 1915

Dear Little Daddy,

(...)

Yesterday as usual, I went up for dressage. Since there was a horse that no one could ride, I offered to ride it.

As soon as I was in the saddle, he made such a leap that I found myself more than 2 meters tall, all four irons in the air, but fortunately without the slightest harm. From there, I brought him to the merry-go-round where I rode him managing to hold myself for 12 terrible nose-ups, but in the end, I fell, leaving one foot caught in the stirrup and being dragged for a few meters, but thanks to my composure I managed to free myself from a kick. I immediately went back upstairs, holding myself fairly well, but as he refused to walk, I thrust his stirrups in. He then stood up with both hands and knocked me down for the third time. Without fear I reassembled it, showing, in front of everyone, that an "Oriental" [93] was not afraid of anything or anyone. I was congratulated by the officers and all the staff of the armoury. When the horse was calmed down, I went out with everyone else to the walk. But as he had just been frightened by a paper that was flying, he made a leap to the side which made me take a nice involuntary bath in the stream we were crossing. I was reassembling it and during a little gallop we fell, with so much bad luck that the poor horse ended up with a broken leg, while I had not had the slightest scratch.

From now on, November 27th will remain a famous date for me: the one when, for the first time in my life, the meanest horse I have ever met, threw me to the ground six times.

(...)

Juan-Carlos

Letter from Juan-Carlos Dupont 9/2/1916

Postal Sector, February 9, 1916

My dear little sister,

(...)

I thank you for your congratulations, but I believe that any "Oriental" would have done the same thing in my place. The war is not expected to last long, with the entry of the United States into the war, it should be over quickly. You can tell my mother the news of my Croix de Guerre, but tell her that I am out of danger and that I have just returned to Tarbes where I was a little sick, but that now I am very well.

(...)

When I arrive in America, I think I'll go there as a French soldier to be able to show the Boches what we're worth. You will excuse my writing, but as the mail is going to leave, I must act quickly, I do not want you to be able to complain about your little brother who has not forgotten you.

Bon-papa must be happy with my decoration. It was for him that I won it. So, as soon as I get to America, I'll bring it back to him, since it was he who advised me to replace him. Of the 20 or so Boches I killed, half were killed in his name, five for "Tío Victor" and five for Papa, so that I have none left for myself, but I will have time to kill others!

---

93 Synonymous with Uruguayan. This term comes from the first official name of Uruguay: Oriental Republic of Uruguay.

As Boche souvenirs, I have a helmet, a rifle, 40 magazines and bullets, a bayonet, 4 grenades. But as I don't want to take too much burden, I'll leave them at Aunt's.

(...)

Juan-Carlos

Letter from Juan-Carlos Dupont 10/2/1916

Postal 168, February 10, 1916

My dearest mother,

(...)

I am still waiting, with a thousand worries, for the papers I asked you for more than a month ago, to be able to leave like Peyrou with 21 days + 15 and a little more leave. I think Bon-papa must be happy with my Croix de Guerre. When I arrive, I will give it to him as a gift and the diploma that goes with it. Being on the front line for 8 months, I had to do a thousand crazy things to be able to win it. As you can imagine, wherever I was, every day I saw death up close, and bullets and shells didn't pass very far from me. But now that I've got what I wanted, I won't do anything more crazy because first of all, I want to leave for America and then we'll see...

(...)

During the leave I spent with Marie-Louise, I was very good. Once again, Aunt found another letter that Marinette had sent me to the front, but things went very well: Aunt didn't get angry and neither did I. My poor Aunt has been played a third time, and I assure you, my dear mamma, her eyes are wide open, but Marinette and I will cheat on her all our lives. Things with Marinette are going very well; and maybe one day.... but who can know the future.

(...)

To talk a little about the war, I will tell you that it is something that anyone who has not been there will never be able to imagine. It's something terrifying and inconceivable. When I return, I will tell you about the most terrible moments.

If I tell you these things it is because I believe that I will no longer go to the line of fire, otherwise I would not have told you anything so as not to alarm you.

(...)

Juan-Carlos

Letter from Juan-Carlos Dupont 28/2/1916

Tarbes, February 28, 1916

My dear old lady,

(...)

I'm still happy and currently I'm jumping and dancing with joy because if we hold out in Verdun, the war will be over in less than 4 months. And as you can imagine from this moment the "Polka del espiante", especially now that I have been able to visit Paris. I am very sorry not to be able to be at Verdun even though it is very

dangerous, but I would not care. Never has there been so much enthusiasm between us, and to give more certainty to my comrades, I read aloud to them the newspapers of America.
   (...)

Juan-Carlos

The letter ends with a naïve but resembling drawing representing Eugenio Dupont and the "Nena", his fiancée.

Letter from Juan-Carlos Dupont 21/3/1916

Tarbes, March 21, 1916

   Mon Cher Papa
   (...)
   Everyone was enthusiastic and waited for the end of the battle on the Verdun front to resume the offensive. In 3 to 4 months, the war will be over and I will be able to return to my "rancho" and my original Uruguayan land. I am in France, but my heart has never ceased to love the land where I was born and if one day I had to shed my blood for it, I would do so with double enthusiasm. When I am alone, I only sing the Uruguayan anthem and other patriotic songs. I still hold a grudge against these hypocrites of Argentine "barrigas agujereadas", their ingratitude and the injustices they commit. But I console myself by saying to myself, "It's war."

Juan-Carlos

   Chau Chau

Letter from Juan-Carlos Dupont 23/3/1916

Tarbes, March 23, 1916

   I'm in my mother
   (...)
   Tarbes is the most boring city in all of France. As for distractions there is absolutely nothing. There are only peasants who do not know how to speak French, and instead of cars or carriages with coachmen, you see only carts drawn by oxen or donkeys, in the middle of the main street of Tarbes, that is to say the street of the "Grands Fossés", in the middle of the calves, cows and sheep and all kinds of animals. As for the main theatre, it cannot even compare with our old cinema "Paris".
   (...)

Juan-Carlos Dupont

   And will cigarettes arrive soon?

Letter from Juan-Carlos Dupont 18/4/1916

La Rochelle, April 18, 1916

My dearest dad
(…)
Why didn't you close the shop and go to Buenos Aires for the wedding of Eugenio and my nice little sister-in-law? On the day of my little brothers' wedding, instead of celebrating it, I ended up in the infirmary because of a kick to the ankle. Fortunately the horse was not shod, otherwise it would have broken my leg. I am now perfectly well, and continue in the training of horses.
You will no doubt be surprised that this letter reaches you from La Rochelle, but I have been there since Friday with several comrades to train horses.
(…)
No more, dear little daddy, receive a "fuerte abrazo" and kisses from the son who has not forgotten you.

Juan-Carlos

Letter from Juan-Carlos Dupont 25/4/1916

La Rochelle, April 25, 1916

« Dear Mommy »
I am writing this letter to tell you that I am in very good health, but the main reason for this letter is to tell you that I am leaving for La Rochelle with 10 comrades appointed at the same time as me to train the American horses that are arriving from Buenos Aires. Our stay should not be very long, it could last from 15 days to two months.
It seems that we are going to be very well, and as we are going to be near the sea, I have asked Aunt to buy me some bathing trunks.
(…)

Juan-Carlos

Letter from Juan-Carlos Dupont 23/5/1916

La Rochelle, May 23, 1916

Dear Little Sister,
(…)
I also inform you that all relations with Marinette have ceased, a good piece of advice is that you never put a single compromising word in your letters that you send me in France to Aunt's address. Indeed, she secretly opens all my letters. Curiosity is the biggest flaw of women.
(…)
Lots of kisses for mom and dad, and you, get thousands of kisses from your little brother who loves you very much

Juan-Carlos

Letter from Juan-Carlos Dupont 7/8/1916

La Rochelle, August 7, 1916

My dear little mamma,
How long do you think you will leave me without a letter from you, or from papa and Potota. I haven't received any letter for almost 2 and a half months.
How long this war is! Who would have thought that it would last more than 2 years? As you can see, it befalls me the sad fate of not having gone to the front yet, although I ardently desire it. But I'm starting to get tired of this lazy life. All the comrades I had on board the Lutetia have been in the trenches for more than a year and a half, while I am ashamed not to be able to share their sufferings. However, if I love France, I love my Uruguay even more. France has never been grateful or generous, on the contrary, I see only an immeasurable amount of great injustices.
(...)
Many kisses to Papa, Potota, Mamaseñora, Nena, and you receive a million kisses from your "negro feo"

Juan-Carlos.

Letter from Juan-Carlos Dupont 29/9/1916

Tarbes, September 29, 1916

My dearest little mother,
(...)
I really want to learn English which would be very useful to me. I'm going to ask Aunt to get me some grammar to study it because I think I'll be able to learn it very easily. Thus I shall know Spanish, French, English and Italian.
(...)

Juan-Carlos

Letter from Juan-Carlos Dupont 4/11/1916

November 4, 1916

My dear little Mamma
As I told you in my last letter, which left Périgny, I am in the city of Amiens. Work, as I told you in my last correspondence, is not very important. I am busy feeding and making the horses drink so that they become strong before sending them to the front.
The front lines were 60 kilometres away and the sound of the cannon barely reached here. So, my dear mamma, I am in no danger, although enemy aeroplanes target us often enough to throw a few bombs at the military installations. Here, "Boche" prisoners arrive every day. I very much regretted not being able to get closer to the front and I had to make do with the sound of the cannon.
The city of Amiens is very pretty, and we have a lot of fun. There are a large number of English people who are very friendly. We sleep on straw in a school. The

food is quite average and the packages you send me will be welcome. Send me a lot of newspapers because I am very bored without having anything to read about my country.

When my comrades ask you if I'm on the front, tell them I am. Indeed, otherwise I will have the shame of being taken for an "ambush". The news of the war is very good. Every day, we move forward, taking hundreds of prisoners. Our English allies are very kind. They love us very much and offer us all they have; That is to say cigarettes, souvenirs and finally something to eat.

It's been a long time since I've received a letter from you. My dear mamma, I will ask you to write to me more often.

With no further news for now, with lots of kisses to Papa, Potota, Mamaseñora and Bon-papa, receive a million kisses and abrazos from the son who loves you very much.

Juan-Carlos

Letter from Juan-Carlos Dupont 1/1/1917

Beauvais, January 1, 1917

My very dear mommy
(...)
My health, as usual, is very good, although I have a bit of a cold in recent days. You tell me that I live a life of a walker in France, but in that you are mistaken. I have now been seven months on the Somme front where, for my courage and volunteering for the most dangerous posts, I was the first to receive the Croix de Guerre and the mention in dispatches. I received my decoration a long time ago, during my first month at the front. The superiors like me very much because I'm barely 18 years old. If you are asked, here is my citation: "Always volunteered to accompany the non-commissioned officer observer in the trenches of the 1st line. Very calm and having a deep disregard for danger. Distinguished himself especially on October 31st and November 1st, 1916". SP on 3 November 1916 - Croix de guerre. Now, my darling little mamma, when you are asked about me, you will be able to tell the truth.

If I hid all this from you, it is because I did not want to hurt you and if I am now telling you the truth it is that I am in Beauvais until February and that as soon as I receive the necessary papers, I will leave for America, on leave. I went out in the Tarbes newspapers and am going to ask Aunt to send them to you.

(...)

Now, dear little mamma, I will tell you that I am going to Tarbes with 15 days' leave as a reward for my conduct under fire.

Without anything else, my dear mamma, receive a million kisses and "abrazos" from your son who loves you very much.

Juan-Carlos

Letter from Juan-Carlos Dupont 4/3/1917

March 4, 1917

My dearest mother,

(...)

I thank you very much for the congratulations you give me for my Croix de Guerre. If I didn't tell you the news before, it's because I was at the front and didn't want to frighten you. To frighten is the word because those who have never been able to see it with their own eyes will never be able to imagine it. We must not think that war is like the war between "Blancos and Colorados". Every day we receive asphyxiating shells or some other types of novelties.

(...)

Juan-Carlos

Letter from Juan-Carlos Dupont 10/3/1917

March 10, 1917

My dearest mother,

When you receive this letter, I will be about to embark for Montevideo.

As soon as I received the papers, I ran to bring them to the office, and now with the favorable agreement of my Battery Captain and that of the Group Commander, they have left for the Minister's signature. It should take a month and then "The Polka of the Departure" for me. How I can't wait to see Montevideo again and especially my mom and dad! I hope to be there before the two months.

My health is still very good. I am now facing the "Boches", but you don't have to worry because they don't fire much anymore, because with each cannon shot, we respond with 5 of our own. They are lost, and before four months the war will be over, we are in fact preparing for them a correction which will throw them out of France and deliver us forever from this German epidemic.

(...)

Juan-Carlos

Letter from Juan-Carlos Dupont 29/4/1917

Langres, April 29, 1917

My dearest mother,

(...)

I am in a hospital in Langres, because of the asphyxiating gas used by the Germans during the recent fighting in Champagne, and which you may have heard about in the newspapers. As I am completely recovered, I will leave Langres next Friday, convalescing thanks to my American nationality.

I'm now going to tell you about my campaigns: when I went to the front for the first time, I had my baptism of fire on the Somme. I witnessed the attacks on Comble, Boucavesnes, Rancourt, Sally Sallisel Bois de St Pierre Wast. Having been relieved by the English, we were at rest for two months. During these fights, we had 65% losses between killed and wounded. I was very lucky, I came close to imminent death in at least twenty circumstances. After a well-deserved rest, we set off again on the Somme, near Montdidier and I had the glory of pursuing the Germans to the town of Ham, an advance of 30 kilometres, via Roye. We were again replaced by the British, but we had no deaths or wounded. I was very happy and proud to have liberated French territory, as well as a few thousand old people, women and children. Unfortunately these bandits of Germans had burned down all the villages and cut down all the trees. From that moment on, my hatred increased and I swear to you that when a German falls into my hands, I will kill him by making him suffer. When we were replaced, we took the train and went to Champagne where I witnessed the first two attacks and having been caught by gas, I went to the hospital in the city of Langres. Here are all the fights I've done. If it is true that I did not have a long time of war, I was present at the main battles and victories.

(...)

France has now changed a lot since the last lead (of 50 kilometers). Everyone is sure of victory. The soldiers who had been in the trenches since the first days were full of courage, while the German prisoners could not stand upright, were as thin as sardines, but what made them suffer most was the knowledge that their families were dying of hunger.

Juan-Carlos

On 18 September 1926, Juan-Carlos Dupont, a personality *"of a tumultuous and rebellious character, courageous, frank and good-hearted"* as he described himself in one of his letters, married Marie-Marguerite Lalanne, known as *"Marinette"*, the princess of his 17th birthday and daughter of Marie-Louise, his father's first cousin, in Tarbes. They had a son and two daughters.

15. The Cestia in France from 1900 to 1946

The Cestia were then present mainly in Bigorre, but also in Aquitaine, in Nay further west south of Pau as well as in Gironde.

The territory designated by Bigorre is that of the former county of Bigorre, which corresponds to a large part of the current department of Hautes-Pyrénées represented in bold on the map below.

At the beginning of the twentieth century, the Cestia were present in several towns and villages in Bigorre. They are most numerous in Lescurry and Vic-en-Bigorre, but they are also present in Artagnan, Dours, Castelvieilh, Lacassagne, Lansac, and Louit. In these towns and villages, they are most often farmers, cultivators and ploughmen.

All the Cestia families living in 1900 in the various towns and villages of Bigorre were not closely related. Bearing the same name, they probably knew each other, but therefore must not have had family relations.

Louit, which is located 2 km from Dours, is the native village of Honoré Cestia.

In Dours lived the Paul Félix Cestia family husband Thérèse Laffargue, a family of ploughmen, who came from Escondeaux, near Lescurry. The Cestia de Dours had been in this village for several generations. A first cousin of Paul Félix, Michel Charles Cestia lived in Castelvieilh and then in Pouyastruc, villages near Dours. The first of Michel Charles' two sons was declared at birth under his mother's name, and then some time later was recognized by his father. Later, he went to live in Bordeaux far from the Bigorre... In 1870, the society did not welcome children born without a father at birth with open arms. His descendants went to settle in Epernay.

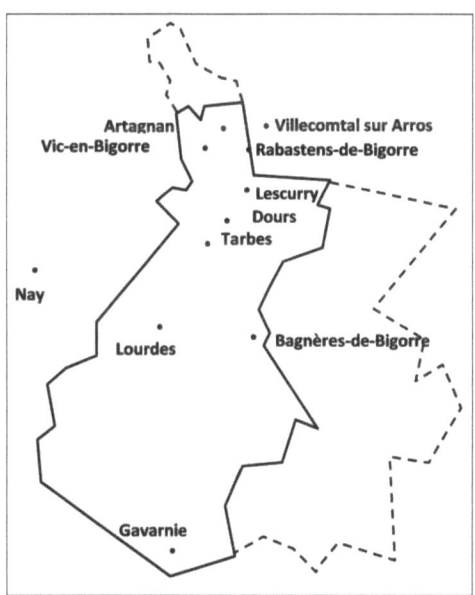

A Lescurry lived in 1900 Jean Cestia and his youngest son Denis Adolphe which in 1886, at the time of the revision council, was classified as *"ancillary service"* because of its too small size. To be a soldier, you had to be at least 1 meter 54 cm tall. But his size did not prevent him from becoming mayor of his commune from 1892 to 1908. There was also a Coutillou family, a Cestia who was called *"Coutillou"*.

> "**The houses** are, so to speak, personified; They are even more important than people: they have a life, a story. The various fortunes of the principal houses of the commune are told; they have a name that is almost never that of the present owner. It is a heritage of which the present generation is merely the custodian, which it holds to its honor not to let wither in its hands, and which it hopes to transmit intact and enlarged to the next generation. Thus inheritances are rarely dismembered, which explains the general derogation within the limits of the law from the equality of division between the children of the same family. The cadets are almost always compensated in money and the paternal inheritance remains mostly intact. »
>
> Monograph Municipal Monograph Study and Research Work Jean-Pierre Bove 1988 Under the direction of M. Michel Papy page 45

Nickname and house name - The use of a nickname was frequent in Bigorre in the eighteenth and nineteenth centuries. This is what Thierry Cenac [] points out[94] in his monograph of the village of Dours, where he indicates that in Bigorre the names of houses are often indicated after the patronymic name in the civil registers. This nickname is sometimes passed on even after the family has left its village of origin, and therefore the house justifying the nickname. House names and family names have variable spellings depending on the priest in charge of writing the act.

The houses of the Cestia are, in Louit, the Baïlou house, in Lescurry the Biuatou houses, Bordenave, Bourdale, Coubé, Coutillou, Dutrey, in Dours the house of Sausette, and in Nay the house of Trébaire.

A Lescurry, Dominique Cestia, the youngest of 6 children, was the son of Denis Damien (1807-1864) a *"Coutillou"*. They are the last to bear this nickname.

A Vic-en-Bigorre in 1900, Alexander's parents and sister Marie Laura left for Louisiana and died. There is therefore only one Cestia family left in Vic, that of Jean Cestia and his wife Dominiquette Setze and their two daughters Paule and Rosina, whom we have already mentioned earlier, the only survivors of a family of 8 children born between 1842 and 1868.

In Castelvieilh lives a Cestia family from Dours, including twins Pierre and Jean. Pierre was a soldier for 5 years while his brother Jean was exempted because he was *"the elder brother of Jumeaux"*.

In Lacassagne lives a family originally from Lescurry.

The Cestia d'Artagnan family is the second generation to live in this small town of a few hundred inhabitants. Grandfather Jean Sestia left Nay to settle in Bigorre.

---

[94] Master's degree in history by Thierry Cenac available on the author's website. http://www.dours.com/

Jean-Marie Sestia's family lives in **Lansac**. Their distant origin is Dours.

Transmission of the surname - The distant ancestors of the Cestia were not always called Cestia. It was the appearance of the family record book around 1877 that made it possible in France to transmit family names without alteration from one generation to the next. In the Nay region, for example, it is customary to double the terminal vowel of surnames.

In Nay there were six distinct families bearing this surname. Families who have been living in these towns for several generations and who, with rare exceptions who have moved to Oloron-Sainte-Marie or Ustaritz, remain there. They are knitters, weavers but also carpenters and cabinetmakers. At the end of the century, they took full advantage of the industrial revolution in this city that journalists of the time called the Little Manchester or the Mulhouse of the Pyrenees. In Nay, in 1852, there were nearly 1,700 textile workers for a population of 4,000 people. But other industries are also present such as furniture manufacturing. Today Nay is known for its Basque beret industry.

> Nay in the nineteenth century
>
> The nineteenth century was the century of the Industrial Revolution, so prosperous for Nay, that the journalists of the time called the city Little Manchester or the Mulhouse of the Pyrenees.
>
> Indeed, some dynamic and ambitious beret manufacturers, led by Prosper Blancq, called on engineers or technicians trained in the best schools of the time to modernize their workshops.
>
> The era of merchants is over, that of industrialists is beginning.
>
> The city's population grew to 4,000 people and there were nearly 1,700 textile workers in 1852.
>
> The factories developed in the city centre itself, a particularity of Nay. One need only mention the Manufacture Blancq, a pioneer of industrial architecture, now transformed into the Beret Museum, or the Berchon Factory with its iron and glass architecture specialising in carded wool, or the Vital Gibert Furniture Factory or the renowned Souyeux Manufacture.
>
> [Official website of the city of Nay]

Cestia and Sestia are also found in the Gironde in Bordeaux, Libourne and Talence, and in the Gers in Villecomtal-sur-Arros.

At the beginning of the twentieth century, Cestia was therefore a much less rare patronymic name in France than it is today.

16. The Cestia in the United States of America from 1900 to 1946

Rosina Cestia was born in 1868 in Vic-en-Bigorre, located a good ten kilometres north-west of Louit. Rosina Cestia has travelled a lot. In 1894 she migrated to New York, then in 1907, she returned from London. In 1920, she married in Vic en Bigorre, her hometown.

On July 27, 1907, Fortunato Cestia, born in Rome in 1889, unmarried, arrives in New York with 12 dollars in his pocket. He made the Naples – New York crossing aboard the Cretic. He left his mother in Rome in the house where he was born in Via San Felice Circeo [95]. He is a farm worker. He could neither read nor write. He came to the United States of America to be with his brother-in-law J. Antonia Armento Payton. On his arrival, he was examined by the doctor H Mc Maste who certified his state of good health.

On September 16, 1910, Serafina Cestia, born in Italy in 1875 in Alcara-Li-Fusi in Sicily, married, arrived in New York with 15 dollars in her pocket. She made the crossing from Palermo. She can neither read nor write. She comes to the United States of America to be with her brother in the *"Carmelia Valenti."*

Pierre Sestia was born in Nay (Pyrénées-Atlantiques) in 1848. He is the son of Jacques Sestiaa de Nay. He was first an employee, then a knitter in the textile industry of Nay and finally a butcher. After the birth of his third child around 1878, Pierre Sestia migrated to the United States in Sausalito, California, where he remained without his children or his wife, who would end her life in Nay.

1917-1918 - Involvement of the USA

When war broke out, the President of the United States wanted to observe strict neutrality. But on the economic and financial level, American neutrality was theoretical because the longer and more total the war became, the more the Entente countries resorted to the United States for supplies but also for borrowing.

The tense situation between Germany and the United States led to the severance of diplomatic relations on 1 February 1917 and the declaration of war on 6 April 1917. On 18 May 1917, the conscription of all male citizens between the ages of 21 and 30 was voted, which increased the number of men in the army from 200,000 in February 1917 to four million in November 1918.

With two million men landing in France, the year 1917 saw the establishment of the war machine of the United States, which, for the first time, intervened in a conflict on a global scale and established itself as a great power.

---

95 North of Rome, 10 to 15 km from the centre of Rome.

How I wish I could tell you why he went so far alone!

But the most numerous Cestia are those of the family of Alexander and his wife Vest Lovina from New Iberia in Louisiana. Alexander was born in Abbeville, Louisiana, to a family originally from Vic-en-Bigorre.

In 1882, following the death of their father, who still owned property in Vic-en-Bigorre, Alexander and his sister Laura who are also resident in New Iberia, do not go to France to receive their inheritance, but they give power of attorney for the sale of a building and a plot of land.

Alexander and Lovina's seven children were born between 1880 and 1899. They now have a large number of descendants in the United States, especially in Louisiana, whose existence can be followed thanks to Facebook…

Of Alexander's seven children, four were involved in the European conflict of the First World War: Harry Paulin, Oley Burton, Georges Clayton and Alphe Bruce. All four of them returned safe and sound, but also participated in 1942 [96] to the second conflict with Germany alongside four of George Clayton's children: Fabian, Claude, Donald and John.

Perhaps they had forgotten, or perhaps not, that they were defending the soil of their ancestors. They probably did not know that they were fighting alongside the Cestia of France.

---

96 In 1942, the United States reinstated conscription. They mobilize 12 million men and women.

17. Conclusion

This is the story of the Cestias. The story of lives that are based on encounters, opportunities, chance but also on the desire to control one's destiny.

This trip made us meet people who, quite simply, have made history of which we are just the continuity. It is we who make history today. But can what we are today escape the influence of past generations? I don't think so. Society's current demand for respect for human rights is only possible because those who preceded us have conquered, step by step, all the levels of human rights. Our freedom is the one that was gradually won in the nineteenth and twentieth centuries. We make history today, but history today makes us.

Over the course of the pages, we have met lives that have sometimes been oriented by chance. Because no one can decide to be born in a chosen place and time, to be born French, or American, to draw the right number so as not to go to war, to be healthy or fragile, etc.

But lives that are also the fruit of the will to win. Overcoming food shortages, famines, the will to survive in the face of epidemics. We have crossed destinies that are the result of the courage to go to the other side of the world to realize our dreams, our ambitions, to become a notable of our village or the one we admire because he defeated the enemy, or also sometimes more simply to get out of misery.

In a nutshell, the lives we met during this journey are in the end, modestly, the result of a paradoxical mixture, made up of chance and willpower.

18. Alphabetical index of individuals cited

The index refers to the page number. On each individual cited, detailed information, and sources are available on http://www.genea-cestia.fr/

abaresJeanne F............................. 72
Abbadie Marie 26
Adamet Marie 27
Adamet Marie, ... 29
Ader Jeanne Marie 97
Adnet Jean Joseph Marie Eugène (1822-1900) 99
Ageville 69
Anglade Marie............................... 27
Anglade Marie............................... 26
Aquart Modestine......................... 77
Aquart-Pieton Marie Cécile Eugénie 77
Aquart-Pieton Marie Cécile Eugénie 19
Bachelier 70
Baïlou 146
Baron Marie 27
Becas Geneviève Jeanne............... 80
Bernis Gabrielle............................. 41
Bicata Jacques Frechou 48
Bire Anne............................... 52, 97
Biuatou....................................... 146
Blon 119
Bordenave 146
Bordere Joseph 67
Bordis Justine 84
Bourdale..................................... 146
Brescon Jean 67, 68
Brescon Jean-Baptiste fils 68
Brescon Jeanne épouse Darré 68
Brescon Jeanne Marie épouse Lamarque...................................... 68
Brescon Marie épouse Dubeau 68
BurguesCatherine Marie................. 66
Candebat................................... 119

Carrere Bertrand........................... 67
Carrere Jean................................. 80
Carrere Jean Pierre 75
Carrere Jean Pierre 75
Castane Houley.......................... 121
Caubet Jeanne............................. 27
Cestia Alberte 118
cestia Alexander 149
Cestia Alexandre, dit Darric 97
cestia Alphe Bruce 149
Cestia André................................. 20
Cestia Antoine 52, 84, 97, 99
Cestia Arnaud 98
Cestia Arnauld 48
Cestia Arnauld Biuata 48
Cestia Auguste Sylvain 91
Cestia Auguste Sylvain 93
Cestia Auguste-Sylvain 18
Cestia Bernard 95, 99
Cestia Bernard époux Lajusa 80
Cestia Bernard et Jacques 99
Cestia Bernard et Jacques 90
Cestia Bernarde 99
Cestia Bertrand.....................71, 100
Cestia Bertrand 19
Cestia Bertrand 68
Cestia Bertrand (1805-1876) 18
Cestia Bertrand (1810-1885) dit le cadet 78
Cestia C 100
Cestia Catherine 20
Cestia Catherine et Pierre 75
Cestia Chiquita 107
Cestia Coutillou............................ 76

Cestia Denis Adolphe 145
Cestia Denis Damien époux Michèle Baru.. 81
Cestia Dominique 146
Cestia Dominiquette Bernarde 85
Cestia Dorothée 99
Cestia Emile................................. 121
Cestia Emile..................... 17, 20, 111
Cestia Émile................................. 104
Cestia Émilio................................ 104
Cestia Felipe................................ 104
Cestia Felix 17, 20, 106
Cestia Fortunato 100, 148
Cestia François 77
cestia Georges Clayton 149
Cestia Giovanni 101
Cestia Giuseppe 101
Cestia Guillaume 17
Cestia Guillaume dit Coubé 47
cestia Harry Paulin 149
Cestia Honoré 92
Cestia Honoré 17, 20
Cestia Honoré 88
Cestia Honoré 104
Cestia Izaure 99
Cestia Jacques Coutillou 27
Cestia Jean........ 84, 96, 100, 145, 146
Cestia Jean...............................16, 75
Cestia Jean.................................... 29
Cestia Jean.................................... 66
Cestia Jean (1792-1867) 97
Cestia Jean Alphe (1834-1860 100
Cestia Jean Alphe (1834-1860) 17
Cestia Jean dit Coutillou 80
Cestia Jean dit Dutrey-Coutillou 42
Cestia Jean Dutrey-Coutillou (1745-1815).. 47
Cestia Jean, dit Jacques 83
Cestia Jean-Alphe 78
Cestia Jean-Marie 84

Cestia Jean-Marie 99
Cestia Jeanne................................48
Cestia Jeanne................................41
Cestia Jeanne (1768-1777). 41
Cestia Jeanne-Marie......................84
Cestia Joseph 97
Cestia Joseph (1847-1871)............99
Cestia Juan 105
cestia Jules 122
Cestia Jules 123, 129
Cestia Jules 17, 20, 104
Cestia Jules,................................115
Cestia Julio..................................104
cestia Laura 149
Cestia Louis..................... 76, 84, 99
cestia Louise (1820-1882)..............79
cestia Lovina 149
Cestia Maria 101
Cestia Marie 85, 100
Cestia Marie Cécile Eugénie épouse François..77
Cestia Marie-Anne........................84
Cestia Martial 72
Cestia Martial 20
Cestia Martial 75
Cestia *Mauricio Mario Honorato*....107
Cestia Michel................................84
Cestia Michel Charles 145
cestia Oley Burton 149
Cestia Paul Bernard 79
Cestia Paul Felix 145
Cestia Paul Hyppolite 84, 99
Cestia Philippe..............................91
Cestia Philippe................... 18, 19, 88
Cestia Philippe............................104
Cestia Philippe dit Bernard 74
Cestia Philippe épouse Carrere 74
Cestia Pierre............... 29, 70, 76, 82
Cestia Pierre..................... 18, 19, 20
Cestia Pierre................................70

Cestia Pierre 70
Cestia Pierre 72
Cestia Pierre 75
Cestia Pierre 82
Cestia Pierre dit Baillou (Bayou) 82
Cestia Raymond 41
Cestia Raymond époux Jeanne Durac
 81
Cestia Rosina 148
Cestia Serafina 148
Cestia Sérafina 100
Cestia Victor 104
Cestia Vincent 99
Cestiaa Jean époux Bergeret 80
Cestiaa Jean époux Bergeret 80
Cestian Anne Biccatan (1756-1756).
 42
Cestian Arnaud 29
Cestian Arnauld (1716-1788) 16
Cestian Arnauld Biuatou (1716-1788
 42
Cestian Arnauld Biuatou (1716-1788)
 42
Cestian Bernard 29, 41
Cestian Bernard (1692-1781) 41
Cestian Bernard (1760-1854) 41
Cestian Bernard (1760-1854) dit
Coubé 80
Cestian Bernard Bourdale 42
Cestian Bernard Saucetter 52
Cestian Bicatan (1743-1743), ... 42
Cestian Claire Biuatou (1718-1761 . 42
Cestian Claire Biuatou (1744-1744) 42
Cestian dit Guillaumet 51
Cestian Etienne Biuatou (1748-1783)
 42
Cestian Etienne dit Biuata (1748-
1783), ... 48
Cestian Guilhaume 51
Cestian Guilhem 29
Cestian Guillaume 41
Cestian Guillaume 41
Cestian Guillaume époux Marthe
Dumestre 81
Cestian Guillaume et Bernard......... 41
Cestian Jean 41
Cestian Jean 24, 29
Cestian Jean 50
Cestian Jean Bicata 24
Cestian Jean Bicata (1667-1731).... 41
Cestian Jean Coubé 99
Cestian Jean Coubé 52
Cestian Jean dit Coubé 84
Cestian Jean dit Guilhaumet 29
Cestian Jean dit Guilhem 51
Cestian Jean dit Sausette 52
Cestian Jeanne Marie 52
Cestian Jeanne Marie (1745-1794). 47
Cestian Marie 27, 29
Cestian Marie (1697-1762 42
Cestian Marie Biccatan (1751-1753)42
Cestius 14
Clemens Catherine 24
Costabadie Jean 22
Cotin 69
Coubé 146
Coutillou 146
d'Esparos Géraud 15
dametMarie A 51
Dardenne Jeanne 29
Darre Marie 85
Darric Jeanne 22, 24
d'Astarac Jean 15
d'Astarrac Jean 15
Daubes Domenge 99
Daveran Dominique 79
de Comminges Cécile 15
de Fougères Raveil, ... 69
de Podenas Philippe 22
de Sestias Condorine.................... 15

Alphabetical index of individuals cited

de Sestias Guillaume 15
Dedieu Joseph 100
Desbordes Pierre 68
Despalanques 69, 80
Despalanques Jean 66, 99
d'Esparros Géraud......................... 15
Dortignac Abraham 89
Dortignac Madeleine 93
Dortignac Madeleine Marthe 105
Dortignac Magdelaine..................... 75
Dortignac Magdelaine..................... 19
Dortignac Magdelaine..................... 74
Duco Bernard 47
Duffau Jeanne 84
Duffau Marie 84
Dulac Domenge 99
Dumestre Marthe 41
Dumornay Matignon Marie Anne Zeline................................... 72
Dumornay-Matignon Marie-Anne-Zeline................................... 19
Dupont Domingo 129, 131
Dupont Domingo 105, 125
Dupont Dominique 92
Dupont Dominique 91
Dupont Dominique 131
Dupont Graziella 93
Dupont Juan-Carlos...... 132, 136, 139
Dupont Juan-Carlos 20, 105, 120, 124, 129
Dupont Juan-Carlos..................... 142
Dutrey.. 146
Fabares Jeanne 18, 20
Fabares Martial 66, 74
Fabares Martial 18
Fabares Pierre 72, 74
Fontan Jacques............................. 27
Fontan Jacques............................. 29
Fontan Jacques............................. 29
Fontan Marie 82

Fontelieux Marie Zulma 100
Frechou Jacques............................48
Gardey Adolphe.............................85
Gardey Bernarde 24
Gardey Marie.................................84
Gardey Marie.................................27
Gauthier Fernande.......................111
Giorgi Ange Toussaint....................76
Giorgi Ange Toussaint....................20
Gouaille Jeanne Marguerite Anne....26
Gouailles Jeanne marguerite Anne..27
Gouailles Jeanne Margueritte Anne .49
Guilhaume Sestian époux Darric 79
Guillaume.....................................41
Guillemat 72
Guinle Françoise Jeanne 94
Guinle Marguerite 51
Guinle Marguerite 29
J Abadie eanne..............................22
Jammes Jean-Baptiste 71
LafargueJeanne épouse Bonnet......68
Laffargue Bernard et Anne 68
Laffargue Marie.............................68
Laffargue Thérèse 145
Laffont Jeanne 26
Laforgue Marguerite 22, 24
Lalanne Jean.................................48
Lalanne Léon...............................118
Lamon Marie.................................51
Laurens Julie...............................111
Lecurieux Felix 69
Lespiau Anne Marie 22
Louise Catherine...........................42
Luit Marie.....................................51
Luit Marie.....................................29
Luit Marie.....................................51
Marie épouse Laffargue 68
Meyranx Eugène............................92
Meyranx Eugénie...........................92
Moirtin 69

Montbartsier	22
Morand	70
Mothe Jean Jules	88
Mothe Victorine	88
Nougues François	85
Payton Antonia Armento	148
Pehourtic Anne	23, 26, 27, 49
Pére Domengea	29
Philippe Cestia	73
Pieton Eugène Hubert	77
Poineau	121
Pujo Pascal	68
Pujo Paul	78
Rangoni Marquise Andrée del Castel Crescente	108
Richaud Etienne	68
Roques Dominiquette	99
Saux Jean Pierre Felix Victor	73
Sénac Simone	88
Sentubery Dominique	88
Sentubery Jean	88
Sentubery Jean	90
Sentubery Marie	41
Sentubery Marie-Louise	117
Servient François	68
Sestia Jean	84, 85, 99
Sestia Jean	26
Sestia Jean époux Abbadie	79, 80
Sestia Jean Pierre époux Poey	79, 80
Sestia Jeanne Marie	97
Sestia Pierre	148
Sestiaa Bernard	79
Sestiaa Jacques	148
Sestiaa Jean	26
Sestiaa Jean	40
Sestiaa Jean (1787-1849),	94
Sestiaa Jean époux Barthes	79
Sestiaa Jean époux Mesplet	79
Sestiaa Jean Paul (1802-1874)	94
Sestiaa Jean Pierre (1780-1855)	94
Sestiaa Laurent	79
Sestiaa Pierre (1783-1844)	94
Sestiaa Pierre époux Pardilhon	79
Sestian Arnaud	27, 51
Sestian Arnaud	29
Sestian Arnaud (1635-1681) dit Berne	22
Sestian Arnauld	11
Sestian Bernard	11
Sestian Bernard	23
Sestian Bernard	23
Sestian Bernard (1646-1691) dit Camus	22
Sestian Coutillou Guilhem	24
Sestian Coutillou Jean	24
Sestian Coutillou Jean (1636-1726)	22
Sestian Guilhaume	11
Sestian Guilhaume (1642-1726) dit Bernis	22
Sestian Guilhaume époux Darric	79
Sestian Guilhem	11
Sestian Guilhem (1638-1713)	22
Sestian Jean	49, 85, 99
Sestian Jean	22
Sestian Jean	27
Sestian Jean	80
Sestian Jean Bordenave	27
Sestian Jean dit Gouailly	26
Sestian Jean époux Anglade	79
Sestian Jean époux Gouailles	79
Sestian Jeanne dit Peyrou	21
Sestian Joseph	27
Sestian Pierre	22
Sestian Pierre	22
Sestian Pierre et Jean	41
Sestian Pierre Jean	11, 16
Sestian Pierre Jean	22
Sestian Pierre Jean	27
Sestian Pierre Jean	40
Sestian Pierre Jean Dauveille	23

Sestian Pierre Jean dit Dauveille ... 26, 49
Sestian Pierre Jean époux Pehourtic 79
Sestiant (avec un t final) Anne (1748-1808) 80
Sestias 15
Sestias Condorine 15
Setze Dominiquette 96, 146
Sextia 51
St Pierre Jean-Baptiste Philibert 73
St Ubery Anne 51
St Upery Anne 52